BRAISES *AND* STEWS

BRAISES *AND* STEWS

EVERYDAY SLOW-COOKED RECIPES

BY TORI RITCHIE

Photographs by Ben Fink

CHRONICLE BOOKS
SAN FRANCISCO

This Chronicle Books LLC edition published in 2007.

ISBN 10: 0-8118-6055-8
ISBN 13: 978-0-8118-6055-0

Manufactured in China

Designed by Gretchen Scoble Design
Food and prop styling by Melissa Hamilton
Assistant food styling by Julia Lee

Distributed in Canada by
Raincoast Books
9050 Shaughnessy Street
Vancouver, British Columbia V6P 6E5

10 9 8 7 6 5 4 3 2 1

Chronicle Books LLC
680 Second Street
San Francisco, California 94107

www.chroniclebooks.com

This book is dedicated to **Sue Ritchie** for raising me on pot roast and to **San Francisco**, my beloved hometown and the best place to test braising recipes all year;

To **Leslie Jonath** for her endless enthusiasm and love of braised cabbage, to **Laurel Leigh** for her unflappability, to **Ann Martin Rolke** for her careful and thoughtful editing, to photographer **Ben Fink**, food and prop stylist **Melissa Hamilton**, and designer **Gretchen Scoble** for making the pages beautiful;

To **Amanda Haas**, recipe tester, friend, and great company in the kitchen;

To **Mary Risley** for providing her kitchen, useful advice, and good humor;

To those who contributed recipe ideas and inspiration: **Katherine Cobbs**, **Naneita Cobbs**, **Judy Custer**, **Vicky Kalish**, **Sara Whiteford**, and **Susan Herrmann Loomis**;

To **the Hunters**, once again, for the pool house kitchen;

To my culinary gal pals, who keep me laughing and excited about what we do: **Julie Hamilton**, **Katherine Cobbs**, **Donata Maggipinto**, **Sara Whiteford**, **Mary Barber**, **Bibby Gignilliat**, **Kelly Whalen**, **Diane Morgan**, and **Sara Deseran**;

To **Brooks-An Brazil** for supplying great chile peppers from Santa Fe;

To **Blaise**: You know why you have to be in this book;

And, most of all to **Sam Whiting**, who eats everything.

contents

INTRODUCTION

A big yellow pot is on the stove, there's a warm fire underneath it, and an incredible scent fills the air: There's pot roast for dinner and everyone is hanging around the kitchen. This is why we braise, because who can resist lifting the lid off that pot and dipping in to the tender meat, vegetables, and sauce below? Braising is primal. If, as it's said, the first cooking method discovered was grilling, I have to believe the second was braising. It's also global. Italians will swoon over *stracotto,* their pot roast; the French have elevated braised fish to art with bouillabaisse; Mexican carnitas has fueled generations from the Yucatán to the Yukon; and Indian curries have influenced empires. Yet braising is uniquely local, too. Every cook seems to have a special recipe. Isn't your mother's (or grandmother's or uncle's) brisket, chili, or ragù the best you've ever had?

What makes braising relevant today is the reason it's been around so long: It's time efficient, economical, alchemical. You can throw food in a pot and walk away for hours while inexpensive, tough cuts of meat and knobby vegetables are magically transformed into dinner. And even though these dishes are "slow-cooked," that doesn't mean they take forever. Putting together a good braise rarely takes more than half an hour, then it needs little attention. Meat braises cook for a couple of hours, poultry takes as little as thirty-five minutes, and seafood and vegetable braises are often done in twenty minutes. Slow is relative; it depends on the type of food you are cooking, not on the clock. Stewing is braising's fraternal twin—made the same way, but with slightly different looks. A stew may have smaller pieces of food and a bit more liquid, but the technique is the same.

To survey all the braises and stews of the world would exceed what I want to do in this book. What I want to do is help you get a great dinner on the table tonight without searching for special ingredients, without exhaustive preparation, without spending a lot of money. These recipes are my favorites, culled from twenty years of loving to experiment with braising. This is everyday food—good for family dinners, good for parties, good for you.

BRAISING BASICS

The word *braising* sounds more technical than it is. The method is very simple: Food is simmered in minimal liquid in a closed pot until the essence in every ingredient flavors every other ingredient. To do it, you have to have the right equipment; you have to know the basic steps; and you have to choose the right ingredients.

THE POT

It doesn't get any more fundamental than this: You need the right pot for braising. It has to be heavy enough for long cooking without scorching; it has to be large enough to hold multiple ingredients, but not so big that they swim around; it has to have a tight-fitting lid so the food can baste over and over in its own juices.

The best all-purpose pot for the recipes in this book is a Dutch oven—a heavy, cast-iron pot with two loop handles and a matching lid. These pots heat up slowly, then retain and distribute heat exceedingly well. The best brands have bumps or spikes underneath the lid, collection points for steam which then drips back down into the food, reinforcing the cycle of flavors. Enameled-iron versions of Dutch ovens don't require seasoning and they come in peppy colors that you will be happy to see on your stove. They can be expensive, but they'll last forever.

Cladded stainless-steel, copper, or cast-aluminum versions of Dutch ovens may be labeled "soup pot," "stockpot," "round oven," or, simply, "braiser." Look for ones that are heavy and durable, with an aluminum or copper core to conduct heat, and a matching lid. I cannot stress enough how important it is that the pot's lid fits snugly, but this varies from manufacturer to manufacturer. If the lid jiggles when you are braising, cover the top of the pot with foil, then place the lid over the foil, pressing down to secure the seal.

As a traditionalist, I think every home needs at least one 5- to 7-quart Dutch oven, and that's the most common pot called for in this book. The reason for the range is that different manufacturers use different sizing. My two favorite brands of enameled-iron pots—Le Creuset and Staub—are made in France and converted measurements can be awkward (like 7.25 quarts). Don't worry about that. A pot in this size range, that measures about 10 inches across, will cover almost every braising need. If you can afford it, a selection of different sizes and shapes, such as oval (perfect for chickens), will make braising even more fun.

A few other pans are useful, too. A wide (10- to 12-inch) sauté pan is good for braising many things, such as vegetables and fish. I recommend anodized aluminum or cladded stainless steel that is heavy bottomed and has a tight-fitting lid. Another pan I use for some braises, like quick curries or shrimp, is a flat-bottomed wok (with a lid). Even though these are meant for stir-frying, the good-quality ones work well for the quick browning and stove-top simmering of a lighter braise. The tapered shape means the surface area is wide, which encourages evaporation and concentration of flavors. Nonstick ones are a snap to clean.

GOING DUTCH

The word "Dutch" in the term *Dutch oven* is said to have come from pots used by the Pennsylvania Dutch (who were actually Germans) in the 1700s. The "oven" part of the name came from placing the vessels, which originally had feet, in the embers of the hearth, then topping the lid with more coals (old-fashioned Dutch ovens have lipped lids) to create the all-around heat of an oven before ovens were commonplace in homes.

The other tools that you need to braise you probably already have in your kitchen: long tongs to turn meat while browning; wooden spoons to scrape the bottom of the pot; oven mitts to carry the pot safely; and a ladle to dish out hearty portions. Add in measuring cups and spoons and a sharp, heavy knife, and you are good to go.

STEPS TO BRAISING

Braising is as simple as cooking long, slow, and low so that each flavor in the pot gradually merges with the others, creating a savory whole far greater than its parts. The food may be browned first, then the pot deglazed, but the ingredients are always simmered, never rushed. Meat and poultry braises and stews have a few other steps, too, which are outlined here.

1. RINSING. *To wash away bits of bone or blood from meat or poultry, rinse with cold water, then pat dry with paper towels. This gets rid of excess moisture so the food will brown well; if it's wet, it won't sear. However, don't rinse meat before flouring it; just pat dry after removing from the package.*

2. SALTING. *It is important to salt food before browning it. The salt will immediately start to penetrate the surface, releasing the first layer of flavor, especially if you use kosher salt (see page 16). Plus, if you get distracted and forget to salt later on in cooking, you can be assured that some seasoning is already in the pot. Even when onions are the first ingredient browned, it's a good idea to salt them to start coaxing out flavor.*

3. DREDGING. *Traditional braises often included the step of flouring meat to thicken the sauce. Today, braises tend to be made with less liquid, so that the sauce thickens through reduction (which also concentrates flavor). There aren't many recipes in this book that include flouring, but it is essential for a few, and the best method is to spread all-purpose flour on a piece of parchment or waxed paper and toss the meat in it. Then, in batches, put the floured pieces in a mesh colander and shake off the excess (if there's too much flour it will scorch in the pan).*

4. BROWNING. *Meat and poultry braises often start with browning, which adds incredible depth to the sauce, but must be done with attention. First, coat the pot with just enough oil to spread a thin film over the bottom when the pot is tilted. Then heat the pot until the oil shimmers, but doesn't smoke, and sizzles robustly when a piece of food hits it. Be patient getting to this point: If the oil isn't hot enough, you will never get the caramelization that gives the braise backbone.*

Next, add some meat to the pot, but don't fill the bottom tightly; you should have a little airspace between pieces. If you pack the food in, you'll drop the temperature of the oil so quickly the meat will just steep in its juices; it's always better to brown in batches. Wait until the meat isn't sticking to the pot anymore; at that point only *should you turn it. Keep a plate handy and transfer the browned pieces to it with tongs (juices will accumulate as the meat sits, so a plate captures them). The tongs keep your hand and arm a safe distance from splatters and they don't pierce the meat like a fork would, letting the juices drain out.*

5. DEGLAZING. *When the last batch of browned meat is removed, it's time to either pour in broth, water, or wine to deglaze the pot and loosen those caramelized bits sticking to the bottom. Use a wooden spoon to scrape them up without scratching the pot. If you are adding aromatics like onions or celery first and the pot starts to scorch, add a half cup or so of water, even if the recipe doesn't say so; this will deglaze those bits and the water will evaporate so the vegetables still can be sautéed.*

6. SIMMERING. *Braises are always simmered, but what does simmer really mean? If it is too vigorous, it will toughen meat. If it is too slow, the flavors will never meld. The right simmer should be a few little bubbles at a time breaking the surface of the liquid; it shouldn't be bubbling madly. Once you've reduced the heat under your pot to a simmer, wait about 10 minutes, then check; you may need to adjust the flame to maintain a steady, gentle pop pop pop. Every stove and every pot will simmer at different rates.*

THE CUTS OF MEAT

Braising requires a brief anatomy lesson: The cuts of meat most often used are tough and sinewy, including the shoulder, leg, and flank. (Tender muscles, such as the loin, should be sautéed, grilled, or roasted, but not braised.) These muscles have lots of collagen in the connective tissue, which breaks down through long,

slow cooking into gelatin and gives body to the sauce. Slow cooking also releases the gelatin in the bones; when the sauce is chilled, it gels. That's the richness that makes braises so good. Since animals are butchered differently in different parts of the world (and even in the U.S.), and cuts can be called different names in different areas, here is a simplified list of what is used in this book.

BEEF

BRISKET is a braising classic; it's also the cut used for corned beef and a lot of great barbecue. It is big and meaty and relatively lean. The whole brisket tapers slightly and different butchers tend to break it down into different parts. In general, the front-cut or flat-cut is the most widely available. Brisket can be used instead of chuck for pot roast.

CHUCK comes from the shoulder and neck area and has lots of fat and connective tissue, which is why it makes the most tender pot roasts and stews. Chuck roasts can be bone-in or boned, but I find boneless easier to use and more widely available, so that is what I call for in this book. Chuck roasts can be cut to various sizes, but 3 to 4 pounds is perfect for a family meal. I always use boneless chuck for stew; I find "lean beef stew" (usually rump or top round) sold in many meat cases just too dry.

THICKENING SAUCES

Most contemporary braises and stews do not call for flouring the meat to thicken the sauce. If you want a thicker sauce, here are a few ways to do it at the end of cooking:

• Stir in a "slurry" of cornstarch, arrowroot, or potato flour moistened to a paste with water, and cook for a few minutes.

• Knead 1 tablespoon each of butter and flour together, stir into the sauce, then cook for a few minutes.

• Remove meat from pot with a slotted spoon and reduce the sauce over high heat.

SHORT RIBS are layers of meat and fat attached to a wide bone. They are divine when braised. Short ribs are sometimes sold boneless, but that will shortchange the sauce, so I always use bone-in short ribs. Occasionally I ask the butcher to saw or crack the ribs into pieces to make them easier to handle. You can also find 3-bone center-cut short ribs, which are sometimes labeled "kosher" or "Korean-style."

LAMB

The SHANKS and SHOULDER meat make superb braises. Lamb stew from the shoulder comes bone-in and boneless. Bone-in stew makes a more flavorful sauce, but I find it harder to eat, so in this book I call for boneless lamb stew. The shanks need to be braised for several hours; then they are among the most popular of all braised dishes.

PORK

The SHOULDER is best, but it can go by several names, including pork blade shoulder, pork butt, Boston butt, and Boston shoulder. Any butcher will know what you want if you ask for pork shoulder. Bone-in shoulder makes the world's best carnitas; the stew meat is used boneless. I find that ethnic markets are a great source for pork for braising.

VEAL

Both SHOULDER and LEG cuts can be braised. I prefer meat from the shoulder for stewing and boneless, tied leg roasts to braise whole. Braised osso buco, or veal shanks, are among the finest of braised dishes; they are also among the most expensive, but worth it.

Another advantage of braising is that it's very forgiving; because of the slowness of the process, a few extra minutes (even more for meats) won't overcook the dish. When meat braises are done, it's actually a good idea to let them sit before serving to settle the flavors and cool down a bit. The double benefit is that if you wait to serve a braised dish the next day (or eat the leftovers then), it will taste even better (seafood braises are the exception). That's why braises are so convenient for family meals and parties. You can have the finished main dish sitting on the stove, ready to go when everyone else is.

CHILL IT

Most meat and poultry braises taste even better the second day, and if you are particularly concerned with fat, you *should* make them a day ahead so you can chill the cooked food, then lift off the fat. Having an assortment of plastic or glass storage containers with snap-on lids, especially in larger sizes such as 2 quarts or more, will make it more convenient to do this and to store leftovers.

BEYOND BRAISING

All braises come with a built-in sauce, so naturally, you need something to soak it up. Osso buco and risotto are a classic pair; pot roast and mashed potatoes may be the sentimental favorite. To give you an idea of what to serve with your braised dish, there's a whole chapter on accompaniments (page 115). But what goes underneath chili or stew or short ribs isn't the only way to complete your meal; lots of people like to sprinkle something on top. I've included recipes for condiments like horse-radish sauce and seasoned salt and the indispensable Southern staple, hot-pepper vinegar, in this chapter, too. You can also see pairing suggestions at a glance with the chart on pages 136–137. So, mound up the potatoes, ladle on the stew, splash with the final touch, and enjoy.

A NOTE ON INGREDIENTS

As with all cooking, good ingredients are essential for great results. Most things in this book can be bought at a well-stocked supermarket. When I have used specialty ingredients (like custom-blended chili powder), I have given you a source for it, as well as an easy alternative. But a few ingredients are so crucial and used so often, it's important to clarify them here.

BROTH

I have called for "chicken (or beef or vegetable) broth" rather than stock in this book because I believe more people will use canned broth than homemade stock, even though homemade will give the best flavor. Every recipe that calls for broth has been tested with a low-sodium purchased variety. When a recipe calls for beef broth, it *must* be low-sodium (the full-strength stuff is outrageously salty). Fish *fumet* or broth is not called for in this book because it must be made fresh; I don't like the bottled clam juice alternative some cooks recommend. Vegetable broth is a better alternative.

BUTTER

I prefer unsalted butter because the flavor is creamier and I like to control the salting of my dishes. If you prefer regular butter, go ahead and use it.

OIL

Two kinds of oils are called for in this book: vegetable oil and olive oil. Vegetable oil means any light, neutral oil, such as canola, safflower, corn, or blended "vegetable" oil (peanut oil is too strong). Olive oil means a good-quality golden or green olive oil with olive flavor; don't use "light" olive oil—it has no discernible taste. If a recipe calls for extra-virgin olive oil, that is because its unique taste is part of the dish. There are many affordable extra-virgin olive oils now, so you don't have to buy an expensive boutique brand for these recipes.

ONIONS

Without some member of the onion family, braises would taste flat. When I call for a red, yellow, or white onion, but don't specify the size, I mean a medium-size one that weighs about 6 ounces. If yours is a little bigger or a little smaller, don't worry; it won't ruin the dish. Green onions are wonderful in quicker-cooking braises; be sure to use both the white and green parts. Shallots are the underused wonders of the onion family, but some people are perplexed when they peel a shallot and find two lobes. That's why I call for "whole shallots" so it's clear that you use the whole thing, whatever you find under the peel. Leeks have a mild flavor perfect for seafood and other braises. When used, I give directions for cleaning them, as they can be gritty.

SALT

I have only one hard and fast rule in my kitchen: Using kosher salt—as opposed to iodized or regular salt—is a must because the way kosher salt is processed (into flakes), it dissolves quickly in or on whatever you are cooking. Plus if you have kosher salt in a ramekin alongside the stove, it's easy to pinch some up and season the braise as needed.

TOMATOES

Other than onions, tomatoes show up in more braises than any other vegetable, usually in canned form. I like to use organically grown chopped canned tomatoes, such as the Muir Glen brand. Unless the recipe says to drain them, use the juice. If the recipe also calls for water, measure the water in the empty tomato can so you capture the extra tomato juice clinging to the sides. When fresh tomatoes are in season and full of flavor, use them in any braise that calls for canned tomatoes.

Chapter 1

BEEF AND VEAL

Meat braises are the ones many of us craved growing up, the slow-cooked pot roast, short ribs, brisket, and osso buco that made the kitchen smell so good that the family couldn't wait to eat. Many a wise mother chose these dishes because they were filling and inexpensive and usually provided delicious leftovers, too. If those recipes appeal to you, the first step in making them should be to get to know your butcher; the more helpful the butcher, the better your experience with braising beef and veal will be. Shop at a market where you can talk to someone behind the counter who will point out the best cuts and crack the short ribs or trim the chuck. Glean tips from him or her, just like we do from farmers at the weekend market, and your skill with meat braises will grow to the point where you will be creating your own recipes to round out the ones in this chapter.

In the past few years, I cannot believe the number of restaurants serving pot roast as the star entrée. It's funny—I think of pot roast as the ultimate in *home* cooking. My mother's was always made with beer, so I have continued that tradition. The best cut for this is chuck, although it can also be made with brisket. Serve with Herbed Wide Noodles (page 121). [SERVES 6]

classic pot roast with carrots and onions

1 boneless chuck roast (3½ to 4 pounds)

Kosher salt

Freshly ground pepper

Olive oil

2 large onions, chopped

2 large carrots, sliced

2 teaspoons dried thyme leaves

1 bottle (12 ounces) beer

1 cup low sodium beef broth or
   chicken broth

2 tablespoons tomato paste

An hour before starting to cook, remove the meat from the refrigerator, rinse, and pat dry with paper towels. Place on a plate and sprinkle all over with salt and pepper. Let stand to come to room temperature.

Preheat an oven to 350 degrees F. Coat the bottom of a 5- to 7-quart Dutch oven with a thin film of the oil and set pot over medium-high heat. When oil shimmers, put meat in pot and let cook, without moving it, until it is deeply browned on the bottom and lifts easily from the pot when turned with 2 large spoons, about 8 minutes. Do not turn meat with a fork as this pierces it. Continue to brown meat on all sides, turning as needed, about 10 minutes more.

Transfer meat to a plate and set aside. Add the onions and carrots to pot and cook, stirring, until softened, about 5 minutes. Stir in the thyme. Pour in the beer and broth, stirring to release browned bits, then stir in the tomato paste. Let mixture come to a boil, then return meat and any accumulated juices to pot. Cover pot and transfer to the oven. Cook, turning meat over once about halfway through cooking, until meat is tender and pulls apart easily when prodded with a fork, 2½ to 3 hours. Transfer meat to a plate and let rest for 10 minutes; meanwhile, spoon off fat from sauce (if desired, reduce sauce or thicken it as needed; see page 13). Slice meat across grain and serve with sauce and vegetables from pot.

My trusty sidekick on this book, Amanda Haas, grew up eating brisket drenched in homemade barbecue sauce, made by her mother, Jill. This version of that recipe feeds a crowd, so it's a good choice for a party, plus you have to start it the day ahead anyway. Slice meat and serve on buns with Naneita's Coleslaw (page 126), or atop Creamy Baked Polenta (page 117) or cooked grits. [SERVES 8]

braised "barbecue" brisket

4 pounds beef brisket, trimmed
   of excess fat
1 tablespoon chili powder
1 tablespoon paprika
1 tablespoon brown sugar
2 teaspoons kosher salt
1 teaspoon garlic powder
Vegetable oil
1 large yellow onion, chopped

Jill's Brisket Sauce
1 cup water
1 cup ketchup
½ cup packed brown sugar
¼ cup Worcestershire sauce
¼ cup apple cider vinegar
1 teaspoon kosher salt
Freshly ground pepper
Dash hot pepper sauce (or more to taste),
   such as Tabasco

Rinse the brisket and pat dry with paper towels. In a small bowl or ramekin, stir together the chili powder, paprika, sugar, salt, and garlic powder. Rub mixture all over meat, then place meat in a large plastic sealable bag and refrigerate overnight or up to 24 hours.

An hour before starting to cook, remove brisket from refrigerator and let come to room temperature in sealed bag. Preheat an oven to 325 degrees F.

Remove meat from bag. Coat the bottom of an 8- to 10-quart Dutch oven, or other pot big enough to hold brisket in 1 layer, with a thin film of the oil (if you don't have a pot large enough, cut brisket in half crosswise and brown in batches). Set pot over medium-high heat and when oil shimmers, put meat in pot; let cook until it is deeply browned on the bottom and lifts easily from the pot when turned with tongs, 5 to 8 minutes. Turn and brown on other side, 5 to 8 minutes more. Transfer meat to a plate. Repeat with remaining half brisket if necessary.

Add the onion to pot and cook, stirring, until lightly colored, about 5 minutes. Pour in 2 cups water, stirring to release browned bits. Return meat and any accumulated juices to pot, then place a piece of foil over meat, covering to the edges of pot and tucking foil in. Cover pot and transfer to the oven; cook for 2 hours. Remove pot, carefully lift off foil, and turn meat over (if sauce in pan looks dry, add 1 cup water). Replace foil and cover, then return pot to oven.

Continue to cook until meat is fork tender, but not falling apart, about 1 hour more.

Meanwhile, prepare the barbecue sauce. In a saucepan, combine sauce ingredients and bring to a boil, stirring. Remove from heat and let sit until ready to use.

When brisket is tender, remove from oven and discard foil; tilt pot and spoon off as much fat as possible. Pour barbecue sauce over meat, cover pot, and return to oven until meat is very tender and sauce is reduced, about 30 minutes. Remove and let brisket stand 10 to 15 minutes before serving to settle flavors, then slice across grain and offer with sauce.

While most meat braises taste better made the day ahead, this one really *should* be made the day before it's eaten. Because short ribs are fatty (part of why they are so divine), if you chill this overnight, the fat can be lifted right off the sauce. You can also cut the meat off the bones, which makes the dish easier to serve. If you can't find baby carrots, it's fine to use the bagged mini carrots for convenience. Serve these with white or brown rice. [SERVES 4 TO 6]

asian-style short ribs with lacquered carrots

6 short ribs on the bone, about 3 pounds
   total, trimmed of excess fat

Kosher salt

Vegetable oil

1½ cups orange juice

½ cup low-sodium soy sauce

1 teaspoon sugar

1 teaspoon red pepper flakes

1 yellow onion, thinly sliced

2-inch piece fresh ginger, peeled
   and minced

2 garlic cloves, minced

2 bunches baby carrots or 1½ cups
   bagged mini carrots

Preheat an oven to 350 degrees F.

Rinse the short ribs and pat dry with paper towels. Sprinkle with salt. Coat the bottom of a 5- to 7-quart Dutch oven with a thin film of the oil and set pot over medium-high heat. When oil shimmers, add enough short ribs to cover the bottom in 1 layer. Cook, without stirring, until short ribs lift easily from pot with tongs and are well browned on bottom, about 5 minutes. Turn and brown on the other side, about 5 minutes more. Transfer to a plate and continue with remaining short ribs, adding more oil to pot in between batches as needed.

Meanwhile, stir together the orange juice, soy, sugar, and red pepper flakes. Set aside.

When the last batch of short ribs has been removed from pot, drain off all but 1 tablespoon fat and add the onion. Cook, stirring, until onion is softened, about 2 minutes. Add the ginger and garlic and stir 1 minute more until fragrant. Pour in orange juice mixture, let come to a boil, then put short ribs back in pot 1 at a time, bone side up; don't worry if you have to snuggle them a bit.

Cover pot and transfer to the oven. Cook until meat peels easily away from bone when prodded with a fork, 1½ to 2 hours. Remove from oven and transfer meat and bones to a plate. (The recipe can be made ahead to this point; let cool to room temperature and place short ribs and sauce in separate containers and store, covered, in the refrigerator for up to 2 days.)

continued>

If serving the dish right away, cover meat with foil to keep warm. Tilt pot to 1 side and spoon off as much fat as possible from sauce. Place pot over high heat and add the carrots and 1 cup water; bring to a boil. (If made ahead, lift and remove solidified fat from top of sauce. Put sauce in a wide, deep pan, add carrots and water and continue as directed.) Reduce heat slightly and cook, uncovered, at a steady simmer until sauce is reduced by about half and carrots are just tender, 12 to 15 minutes. Return meat briefly to pan to rewarm, then serve. (If reheating meat, cover pan and heat in sauce for about 10 minutes more.)

This recipe was born when I had leftover flat beer from a party Sunday night … what to do with it the next day? Use it in a chili to eat while watching Monday night football and drinking a little more beer, of course. If you don't have stale beer, a freshly opened bottle will do. This is excellent served with Naneita's Coleslaw (page 126) and cornbread. [SERVES 6]

monday night chili

2 dried ancho or pasilla chiles

3 pounds beef stew, preferably chuck, trimmed of excess fat

Kosher salt

Vegetable oil

1 large yellow onion, chopped

One bottle (12 ounces) good-quality beer (fresh or flat okay)

1 medium ripe tomato (about 6 ounces), quartered

2 garlic cloves, peeled

1 yam or sweet potato (about 10 ounces), cut into 1-inch pieces

Garnishes (optional)

1 bunch radishes, sliced

1 cup sour cream

½ cup sliced green onions

Place chiles in a 1-cup measure and cover with boiling water. Set aside to soften.

Cut the meat into 1-inch pieces, rinse, and pat dry with paper towels. Sprinkle with salt. Coat the bottom of a 5- to 7-quart Dutch oven with a thin film of the oil and set pot over medium-high heat. When oil shimmers, add enough meat to cover bottom in 1 layer. Cook, without stirring, until meat lifts easily from pot with tongs and is well browned on bottom, about 5 minutes. Turn and brown on the other side, about 5 minutes more. Transfer meat to a plate and continue with remaining meat, adding more oil to pot in between batches as needed.

When last batch of meat has been removed, add onion to pot, season with a little more salt, and cook, stirring, until starting to color, about 5 minutes. Pour in beer and bring to a boil, stirring to release browned bits, then reduce heat to a simmer.

Lift chiles out of soaking liquid (do not discard liquid) and pull off stems. Split open chiles and rinse under running water to remove seeds. Place the chiles, tomato, garlic, and half the reserved soaking liquid in a blender and purée; add remaining soaking liquid and blend again. Pour mixture into pot; add meat and any accumulated juices and bring to a boil. Cover pot, reduce heat, and simmer 1 hour.

Add yam, nestling into liquid, then cover pot again, and continue to simmer until meat and potato are tender and liquid is thickened, about 30 minutes more. Remove from heat and let stand 5 to 10 minutes before serving, to settle flavors. Spoon into bowls and garnish with radishes, sour cream, and green onions as desired.

I dug an old family recipe for short ribs braised in mustard and beer from my mother's files, then found it tasted much richer with porter or stout (a favorite of mine is Anchor Porter, brewed in San Francisco). Have your butcher cut each rib in two places, so they are easier to handle. Serve with Cheddar Mashers (page 124) or Creamy Baked Polenta (page 117), and more porter to drink. [SERVES 4]

pub short ribs

4 short ribs on the bone,
   about 2½ pounds total, each rib
   sawed into 3 pieces by butcher
Kosher salt
¼ cup whole-grain mustard
1 tablespoon brown sugar
2 garlic cloves, pressed
1 teaspoon red wine vinegar
2 strips thick (butcher) bacon, chopped
1 bottle (12 ounces) porter or stout
Freshly ground pepper
1 large red onion, cut into wedges
1 tablespoon all-purpose flour
1 cup low-sodium beef broth or
   chicken broth

Preheat a broiler to high and an oven to 375 degrees F (if using a separate oven). Line a baking sheet with aluminum foil.

Rinse the short ribs and pat dry with paper towels. Sprinkle with salt. In a large bowl, stir together the mustard, sugar, garlic, and vinegar. Add short ribs and toss with your hands until ribs are covered in mustard mixture. Transfer ribs to foil-lined baking sheet and place in the broiler. Cook until browned on top, about 4 minutes, then turn over with tongs and brown on the other side, about 4 minutes more. (If using the same oven as broiler, set oven temperature at this point to 375 degrees F.)

Meanwhile, put the bacon in a 5- to 7-quart Dutch oven set over medium-high heat. Cook bacon, stirring as needed, until browned, but not completely crisp. Pour off fat. Pour the porter into pot and bring to a boil, stirring to release browned bits.

When short ribs are browned, transfer to pot with tongs. Sprinkle generously with salt and pepper, then scatter the onion wedges over all. Cover pot and transfer to the oven. Cook until meat peels easily away from bone when prodded with a fork, about 1½ hours, stirring contents of pot after an hour.

Transfer pot from oven to stove top and lift out meat and bones with tongs; set aside. Tilt pot to 1 side and spoon off as much fat as possible. (There should be very little sauce in pot at this point; if it is still liquid, place pot over high heat and boil, stirring, until only a few tablespoons remain.) Sprinkle the flour over contents in pot and cook, stirring, over high heat for 30 seconds. Pour in the broth and let come to a boil; cook, stirring, until sauce starts to thicken, about 1 minute. Return short ribs to pot and stir to coat with sauce. Remove from heat and let stand 5 to 10 minutes before serving, to settle flavors.

This is a classic—beef and onions slow-cooked in good wine. I like it with Pinot Noir, although a friend makes a version on Sundays with any leftover red wine from the weekend. While many butchers now sell "lean beef stew" (usually cut from the top round or sirloin), deeply marbled chuck is still the meat of choice for flavor and richness. [SERVES 6]

beef stew with caramelized onions and red wine

3 pounds beef stew, preferably chuck, trimmed of excess fat

Kosher salt

Freshly ground pepper

Vegetable oil

2 tablespoons butter

3 yellow onions, thinly sliced

2 teaspoons sugar

2 tablespoons all-purpose flour

1½ teaspoons dried thyme leaves

1½ cups red wine, such as Pinot Noir

½ cup low-sodium beef broth or chicken broth

1 tablespoon tomato paste

Cut the meat into 2-inch pieces, rinse, and pat dry with paper towels. Sprinkle with salt and pepper. Coat the bottom of a 5- to 7-quart Dutch oven with a thin film of the oil and set pot over medium-high heat. When oil shimmers, add enough meat to cover bottom in 1 layer. Cook, without stirring, until meat lifts easily from pot with tongs and is well browned on bottom, about 5 minutes. Turn and brown on the other side, about 5 minutes more. Transfer meat to a plate and continue with remaining meat, adding more oil to pot in between batches as needed.

When last batch of meat has been removed, add the butter to pot, then the onions and a good pinch of salt, and cook, stirring often, until onions are softened, about 3 minutes. Reduce heat to low and sprinkle the sugar over onions. Cook, stirring occasionally, until onions are limp and golden, about 15 minutes. Stir in the flour and thyme and increase heat to high. Stir 1 minute, then pour in the wine and broth and let liquid come to a boil. Stir in the tomato paste. Return meat and any accumulated juices to pot, let liquid come to a boil, then reduce heat, cover, and simmer until meat is tender when pierced and sauce is thickened, 1½ to 2 hours. Remove from heat and let stand 5 to 10 minutes before serving, to settle flavors.

Way back when, while filming a show about "cowboy cooking," I stopped in at Pendery's spice market in Fort Worth, Texas. I got to play with all sorts of seasonings and I particularly liked the Salt-Free Chile Blend. To order it, go to www.penderys.com. Or use your favorite brand of mild chili powder and adjust the salt accordingly. [SERVES 6]

rich red cowboy stew

3 pounds beef stew, preferably chuck, trimmed of excess fat

Kosher salt

Vegetable oil

1 large yellow onion, thinly sliced

¼ cup mild chili powder (see recipe introduction)

1 can (14½ ounces) chopped tomatoes

Cut the meat into 1-inch pieces, rinse, and pat dry with paper towels. Sprinkle with salt. Coat the bottom of a 5- to 7-quart Dutch oven with a thin film of the oil and set pot over medium-high heat. When oil shimmers, add enough meat to cover bottom in 1 layer. Cook, without stirring, until meat lifts easily from pot with tongs and is well browned on bottom, about 5 minutes. Turn and brown on the other side, about 5 minutes more. Transfer meat to a plate and continue with remaining meat, adding more oil to pot in between batches as needed.

When last batch of meat has been removed, add the onion to pot and cook, stirring, until softened, about 3 minutes. Return meat and any accumulated juices to pot and sprinkle in the chili powder and a pinch of salt. Add the tomatoes and 1½ cups water and let come to a boil; reduce heat, cover, and simmer until meat is very tender, 1½ to 2 hours (check occasionally to make sure liquid doesn't evaporate; if sauce appears dry, add more water ¼ cup at a time). Remove from heat and let stand 5 to 10 minutes to settle flavors, then salt to taste before serving.

Stracotto means "very" or "extra" cooked in Italian, but we might translate it simply as pot roast. I have had stracotto in trattorias and homes in Italy, but this recipe comes by way of an American doctor whose *nonna* made it here, adapting the cut of meat to chuck, a different cut from what they use in Italy. The size of the pot is crucial since the meat braises in its own juice, so test to make sure the pieces fit snugly in one layer; there must be a tight seal, too, so if the lid doesn't fit well, add a layer of foil. Serve Stracotto with Herbed Wide Noodles (page 121) and Horseradish Cream (page 130). [SERVES 4 TO 6]

stracotto

3 pounds boneless beef chuck, in 1 piece, trimmed of excess fat

4 tablespoons extra-virgin olive oil

2 large yellow onions, thinly sliced

1½ teaspoons Lemon-Rosemary Salt (page 133) or kosher salt

Chopped fresh Italian parsley leaves

Preheat an oven to 325 degrees F.

An hour before starting to cook, cut the meat into large chunks, about 4 inches square; rinse meat and pat dry with paper towels. Set aside to come to room temperature.

Pour 3 tablespoons of the oil into a 5- to 7-quart Dutch oven (it should be just big enough to hold meat in 1 layer); tilt pot to coat bottom with oil. Spread half the onion slices on bottom. Top with meat, sprinkle with the salt, then cover with remaining onions. Drizzle remaining oil over all. Cover pot tightly (if your lid isn't a good fit, cover pot with foil, then put lid on top of that).

Place in the oven and cook until meat is literally falling apart, about 3 hours, stirring gently halfway through cooking. Remove from oven and drain off fat. Break up meat slightly with a large fork or spoon. Sprinkle with the parsley and serve.

Because veal is lean and mild, it is wonderful paired with robust ingredients. In classic form, this stew is not browned first, but is thickened with *beurre manié* (butter and flour kneaded together) at the end. To complete the classic picture, offer with Herbed Wide Noodles (page 121) or spaetzle. [SERVES 4 TO 6]

veal stew with marsala and mushrooms

2 pounds veal stew

Kosher salt

Freshly ground pepper

2 strips thick (butcher) bacon

1 tablespoon vegetable oil

1 yellow onion, finely chopped

¾ teaspoon dried thyme leaves

¾ cup Marsala wine

½ cup chicken broth

8 ounces white or brown (cremini) mushrooms, cleaned and sliced

1 tablespoon butter, at room temperature

1 tablespoon all-purpose flour

Cut the veal into 1-inch pieces, rinse, and pat dry with paper towels. Sprinkle with salt and pepper and set aside.

Cut the bacon lengthwise in half, then crosswise into small pieces. Put bacon and the oil in a 5- to 7-quart Dutch oven and set over medium-high heat. Cook, stirring, until bacon is golden brown (but not crisp) and fat is rendered, about 3 minutes. Stir in the onion and thyme and cook, stirring, until onion is softened, about 3 minutes. Increase heat to high and pour in the Marsala; cook, stirring for about 1 minute, to release any browned bits. Add the broth and let come to a boil. Add veal and the mushrooms and cook, stirring, until mixture comes to a boil, then reduce heat, cover, and simmer until meat is tender, about 55 minutes.

Turn off heat under pot. In a small bowl, blend the butter and flour with a fork until paste-like; stir mixture into sauce in pot. Let stew stand, covered, for 5 to 10 minutes before serving, to settle flavors.

Braising meat in milk is an Italian tradition that astonishes most people: It sounds odd, but tastes phenomenal. I first had veal braised in milk in Tuscany, but it is more common in the north. My favorite cookbook in Italian (appealingly called *L'Antichef*, which anyone can translate) includes a variation with vinegar, which inspired me to try it with wine, especially a softer white one might find from northeast Italy. [SERVES 6]

veal braised in milk

1 boneless leg of veal (2½ to 3 pounds), rolled and tied

Kosher salt

Freshly ground pepper

3 tablespoons olive oil

1 small yellow onion, chopped

1 celery stalk, chopped

1 carrot, chopped

½ cup Tocai Friuliano or Riesling

About 2 cups whole milk

An hour before starting to cook, remove the meat from the refrigerator, rinse, and pat dry with paper towels. Place on a plate and sprinkle all over with salt and pepper. Let stand to come to room temperature.

Preheat an oven to 325 degrees F. Warm the oil in a 5- to 7-quart Dutch oven set over medium-high heat. When oil shimmers, put meat in pot and let cook, without moving it, until it is browned on the bottom and lifts easily from the pot when turned with tongs, about 5 minutes. Continue to brown meat on all sides, turning as needed, about 5 minutes more.

Transfer meat to a plate and set aside. Add the onion, celery, carrot, and wine to pot and cook, stirring occasionally, until vegetables are softened and wine is reduced to a few tablespoons, about 5 minutes. Return meat and any accumulated juices to pot, then pour in enough milk to come halfway up sides of meat. Let milk just come to a boil, then cover pot and transfer to the oven. Cook until meat is tender when pierced, about 1½ hours.

Remove pot from oven and transfer meat to plate with tongs. Tent meat with foil and let sauce sit, uncovered, for about 10 minutes (sauce will appear coagulated; this is normal). When sauce has cooled slightly, purée it in a blender (be careful when puréeing hot liquids). Pour sauce back into pot. Clip strings off meat and slice meat into serving portions; ladle sauce over meat and serve.

I love lemon juice and capers with veal scaloppine, so why not with veal shanks? When buying osso buco, you'll see that the shanks range in size. Look for ones that are equal so that they will cook evenly and no one will be jealous of anyone else's portion. Serve over Shortcut Risotto (page 123) and, for an extra zap of flavor, sprinkle with Basil Gremolata (page 134). [SERVES 6]

osso buco with capers and lemon

6 osso buco (veal shanks)

½ cup all-purpose flour

1 teaspoon Lemon-Rosemary Salt (page 133) or kosher salt

2 tablespoons butter

2 tablespoons olive oil, plus more if needed

1 yellow onion, chopped

2 celery stalks, chopped

1½ cups white wine

2 cups chicken broth

2 lemons

3 tablespoons capers, drained and rinsed

Basil Gremolata or chopped fresh Italian parsley leaves

Preheat an oven to 350 degrees F.

Pat the shanks well with paper towels (do not rinse). Dredge shanks in the flour and shake well to rid of excess; sprinkle shanks with the salt. Melt the butter in the oil in the bottom of an 8- to 10-quart Dutch oven over medium-high heat. When foam subsides, add shanks in 1 layer (do in batches if necessary). Cook until crusty and golden brown on the bottom, about 5 minutes, then brown on other sides, turning shanks as necessary with tongs, about 5 minutes more. Transfer shanks to a plate. Continue with remaining shanks, adding more oil to pot as needed.

When all shanks have been removed, add the onion and celery to pot and cook, stirring, until softened, about 2 minutes (if flour starts to scorch, also add ½ cup water and stir to release browned bits). Increase heat to high and pour in the wine; let boil for 1 minute to cook off some of the alcohol. Pour in the broth and let mixture come to a boil, then return shanks to pot. Cover pot and transfer to the oven. Cook until meat peels easily off bone when prodded with a fork, 1½ to 2 hours, turning shanks over once about halfway through cooking.

Transfer pot to stove top and transfer shanks to a plate. Grate the zest of both lemons directly into pot, then squeeze lemon juice and stir it in. Stir in the capers. Taste sauce and season to preference; if necessary, increase heat to high and reduce sauce to desired consistency. Divide shanks among plates or shallow bowls, top evenly with sauce, and sprinkle with gremolata or parsley.

I bumped into a childhood friend one day who had moved to Hungary years before. We had a lot to catch up on, but spent most of the time talking about veal paprikas (pronounced "paprika*sh*"), a dish that's a staple in her home and most others there. This recipe came from that chat. Serve with Herbed Wide Noodles (page 121) or Golden Pilaf (page 118).

[SERVES 6]

veal paprikas

3 pounds veal stew

2 tablespoons butter

2 tablespoons vegetable oil

1 yellow onion, chopped

1 heaping tablespoon sweet
   Hungarian paprika

Pinch cayenne pepper

1 small red bell pepper, finely chopped

1 medium ripe tomato, seeded and chopped

Kosher salt

1 tablespoon all-purpose flour

1 cup regular sour cream

Cut the veal into 1-inch pieces. Rinse meat well in a colander and shake off excess water, but do not pat dry (you want moisture clinging to it). Melt the butter in the oil in a 5- to 7-quart Dutch oven over medium-high heat, add the onion, and cook, stirring, until softened, about 3 minutes. Sprinkle the paprika and cayenne over the onion, then add veal to pot; stir until meat is coated with spices. Reduce heat, cover, and simmer until meat gives off a fair amount of liquid, about 10 minutes. Stir in the bell pepper, tomato, and a generous pinch of salt, then cover again, and cook until meat is tender, about 45 minutes.

In a small bowl, blend the flour with 2 tablespoons water, then stir in the sour cream; stir mixture into pot. Cook, covered, for 10 minutes more. Remove from heat and let stand 10 minutes to settle flavors. Stir well before serving.

Chapter 2

PORK AND LAMB

When we are very hungry, our minds turn to some of the most satisfying foods in the world: shredded *carnitas* in tacos, meaty ragù ladled over pasta, old-fashioned meatballs. What these dishes have in common is that they are made with pork and lamb, meats that were available to even the most humble cook (who had a knack for turning out the richest dishes). That cook would stretch the meat further with local ingredients like beans, tomatoes, corn, greens—even breadcrumbs. Pork, which is naturally mild, supports flavors from assertive chiles to mild-mannered pumpkin. Lamb, widely used from the Mediterranean to India and beyond, shows up with spices and herbs to complement its gamier flavor. The best cuts for braising pork and lamb are the tougher ones—the shoulder, leg, and shanks. It's hard to believe something so homely will become so magnificent in the pot, but just one forkful will prove it.

Poblano chiles are dark green and curvy; if you can't find them, use another fresh green chile, such as Anaheim or New Mexico, or use canned chiles. Because this dish has a soupy texture, it's wonderful ladled over brown or white rice in bowls. [SERVES 6]

pork stew with tomatillos

3 pounds pork stew (from shoulder), trimmed of excess fat

Kosher salt

1 bunch fresh cilantro

1 can (15 ounces) tomatillos, drained

2 fresh poblano chiles, roasted, peeled, and seeded (see page 47) or 1 small can (4 ounces) diced green chiles

Vegetable oil

2 yellow onions, chopped

2 garlic cloves, minced

2 teaspoons ground cumin

2 teaspoons dried oregano leaves

2 cups chicken broth

1 ripe avocado

2 limes

Preheat an oven to 350 degrees F.

Cut the meat into 1-inch pieces, rinse, and pat dry with paper towels. Sprinkle meat with salt and set aside.

Trim root ends off the cilantro stems, then cut off stems and reserve leaves. In a blender or food processor, blend cilantro stems, tomatillos, and chiles until puréed, then set aside.

Coat the bottom of a 5- to 7-quart Dutch oven with a thin film of the oil and set pot over medium-high heat. When oil shimmers, add enough meat to cover bottom in 1 layer. Cook, without stirring, until meat lifts easily from pot with tongs and is well browned on bottom, about 5 minutes. Turn and brown on the other side, about 5 minutes more. Transfer meat to a plate and continue with remaining meat, adding more oil to pot in between batches as needed.

When last batch of meat has been removed, pour off all but 2 tablespoons fat from the pot and add the onions and garlic. Cook, stirring, until onions are softened, about 3 minutes. Add the cumin and oregano, then pour in the broth, stirring to release browned bits. Add the reserved tomatillo purée, meat and any accumulated juices, and 1 teaspoon salt and let come to a boil. Cover and transfer to the oven.

Cook until meat is very tender, about 1½ hours. Remove from oven and let stand 5 to 10 minutes before serving, to settle flavors. To serve, dice the avocado, cut the lime into wedges, and chop a handful of reserved cilantro leaves. Garnish each portion with avocado, lime, and cilantro as desired.

Carnitas is essentially pork pot roast—a chunk of shoulder meat braised until it falls apart. But it is cooked in reverse: First you braise the meat, then you brown it. When buying pork shoulder, it may be labeled "pork blade shoulder" or "pork butt" or "Boston butt" (which seems anatomically confusing, but it is the right cut); just be sure to get a bone-in portion. Roll carnitas into warm tortillas with pickled jalapeños and guacamole, or use it as a filling for enchiladas or tamales, or eat plain with rice and salsa. [SERVES 6]

carnitas

One 4- to 5-pound bone-in pork shoulder
  (Boston butt)
Kosher salt
3 cups chicken broth or water
1 white or yellow onion, quartered
1 tablespoon dried oregano leaves
1 teaspoon cumin seeds
1 teaspoon paprika

An hour before starting to cook, remove the meat from the refrigerator, rinse, and pat dry with paper towels. Sprinkle with salt.

Preheat an oven to 350 degrees F.

Place pork in a 5- to 7-quart Dutch oven and add the broth, onion, oregano, cumin, and paprika. Add a generous pinch of salt. Place over high heat, cover, and bring to a boil; spoon some of the hot liquid over the top of the meat, then cover again and transfer to the oven. Cook until meat is literally falling apart, about 4 hours, spooning liquid over meat once or twice during cooking.

Remove pot from oven and place on stove top. Transfer meat to a platter. With a large spoon, push meat off the bone in chunks; discard bone and any large pieces of fat. Put meat back in pot and turn on heat to medium-high; cook, stirring to break it up with a spoon, until liquid in pot has almost entirely evaporated and meat begins to sizzle, 5 to 10 minutes (the meat should pull into shreds as you work; don't worry if there are some larger chunks). Serve.

Friends of mine in Chicago make big pots of this on fall nights, the red, green, and golden colors of the food matching the trees outside. Use a baking pumpkin—such as Sugar Pie—but not a jack-o'-lantern, which has watery flesh. Or substitute butternut squash (which can often be found precut in produce sections; you'll need about 1 pound in that form). [SERVES 6]

harvest pork stew with pumpkin

2 pounds pork stew (from shoulder),
    trimmed of excess fat

¼ cup all-purpose flour

2 tablespoons paprika

Kosher salt

Freshly ground pepper

Vegetable oil

1 yellow onion, thinly sliced

1 can (14½ ounces) chopped tomatoes

1 bay leaf

1 small pumpkin (about 2 pounds) or
    butternut squash

1 cup frozen, thawed lima beans or
    edamame

1 cup fresh or frozen, thawed corn kernels

3 tablespoons Kat Daddy's Pepper Vinegar
    (page 132) or apple cider vinegar

Cut the meat into 2-inch pieces and pat dry with paper towels (do not rinse). Spread meat on a large piece of waxed paper or the butcher paper it came in. In a small bowl, combine the flour, paprika, a generous pinch of salt, and several grindings of pepper. Sprinkle flour mixture over meat, toss to coat, then shake meat in a colander to rid it of excess flour; do in batches if the colander is small.

Coat the bottom of a 5- to 7-quart Dutch oven with a thin film of the oil and set pot over medium-high heat. When oil shimmers, add enough meat to cover bottom in 1 layer. Cook, without stirring, until meat lifts easily from pot with tongs and is well browned on bottom, about 5 minutes. Turn and brown on the other side, about 5 minutes more. Transfer meat to a plate and continue with remaining meat, adding more oil to pot in between batches as needed.

When last batch of meat has been removed, add the onion and ½ cup water to pot, stirring to release browned bits. Cook, stirring often, until onion is softened and liquid is almost evaporated, about 3 minutes. Add the tomatoes, 1 cup water, and bay leaf and let come to a boil. Return meat and any accumulated juices to pot. Reduce heat, cover, and simmer 40 minutes.

Meanwhile, with a large, heavy knife, cut the pumpkin in half through stem end. Scoop out and discard seeds and strings. Cut pumpkin into chunks, then with a small, sharp knife, pare off the peel. Cut flesh into 1-inch cubes.

After meat has cooked 1 hour, add pumpkin to pot. Let liquid come to a boil, then reduce heat, cover, and simmer 30 minutes more. Stir the lima beans and corn into pot, then cover and simmer until vegetables are cooked and meat is very tender, about 10 minutes more. Stir in the vinegar. Turn off heat and let stand 5 to 10 minutes before serving, to settle flavors.

Pimentón is smoked Spanish paprika. It adds a campfire-like dimension to this dish, but if you can't find it, use regular paprika. Fire-roasted tomatoes with chiles are a wonderful product and the Muir Glen brand is excellent; or substitute regular canned tomatoes mixed with canned diced green chiles. Serve this chili over rice or with quesadillas and Naneita's Coleslaw (page 126). [SERVES 6]

chili colorado with beans

3 pounds pork stew (from shoulder), trimmed of excess fat

Kosher salt

Freshly ground pepper

Vegetable oil

1 yellow onion, sliced

1 red bell pepper, chopped

1 tablespoon ground cumin

1 tablespoon pimentón or paprika

1 tablespoon fresh or 1½ teaspoons dried oregano leaves

½ teaspoon cayenne pepper

1 can (14½ ounces) fire-roasted tomatoes with chiles or 1 can (14½ ounces) chopped tomatoes and 1 small can (4 ounces) diced green chiles

1 cup chicken broth

1 can (15 ounces) pinto beans, drained and rinsed

Preheat an oven to 350 degrees F.

Cut the meat into 1-inch pieces, rinse, and pat dry with paper towels. Sprinkle with salt and pepper. Coat the bottom of a 5- to 7-quart Dutch oven with a thin film of the oil and set pot over medium-high heat. When oil shimmers, add enough meat to cover bottom in 1 layer. Cook, without stirring, until meat lifts easily from pot with tongs and is well browned on bottom, about 5 minutes. Turn and brown on the other side, about 5 minutes more. Transfer meat to a plate and continue with remaining meat, adding more oil to pot in between batches as needed.

When last batch of meat has been removed, add the onion and bell pepper to the pot and cook, stirring, until softened, about 3 minutes. In a small bowl, stir together the cumin, pimentón, oregano, 1 teaspoon salt, and cayenne and add to pot; stir for about 30 seconds until fragrant. Add the tomatoes, broth, and meat and any accumulated juices to pot and let come to a boil. Cover and transfer to the oven. Cook for 1 hour, then stir in the beans, cover again, and cook until meat is tender, about 30 minutes more. Remove from oven and let stand 5 to 10 minutes before serving, to settle flavors.

Here's the dish to make when fresh New Mexico or Anaheim green chiles come into season in late summer or early fall. You can substitute canned green chiles, but the taste will be milder. You can also stir in a large (29-ounce) can of hominy, drained and rinsed, at the point where you turn off the heat and let the stew sit. Or, serve with Golden Pilaf (page 118). [SERVES 6]

true chili verde

1 pound New Mexico green chiles or
   1 large can (7 ounces) and 1 small can
   (4 ounces) diced green chiles
3 pounds pork stew (from shoulder),
   trimmed of excess fat
Kosher salt
Vegetable oil
1 large yellow onion, finely chopped
½ bunch fresh cilantro, leaves and stems
   minced (about 1 cup), plus additional
   leaves for garnish
2 garlic cloves, minced
3 cups chicken broth
1 lime, cut into 6 wedges

If using fresh chiles, preheat a broiler and place the chiles on a baking sheet or large piece of foil. Broil, about 4 inches from the heat, until charred and blistered all over, turning once or twice with tongs. Transfer chiles with tongs to a plastic bag, close bag, and let chiles steam until cool enough to handle. Pull off and discard skins, stems, seeds, and ribs. Chop chiles finely. (Wash hands carefully after working with chiles or use gloves.) Set chiles aside.

Cut the meat into 1-inch pieces, rinse, and pat dry with paper towels. Sprinkle meat with salt. Coat the bottom of a 5- to 7-quart Dutch oven with a thin film of the oil and set pot over medium-high heat. When oil shimmers, add enough meat to cover bottom in 1 layer. Cook, without stirring, until meat lifts easily from pot with tongs and is well browned on bottom, about 5 minutes. Turn and brown on the other side, about 5 minutes more. Transfer meat to a plate and continue with remaining meat, adding more oil to pot in between batches as needed.

When last batch of meat has been removed, stir the onion, minced cilantro, and garlic into pot; cook, stirring, until soft and fragrant, about 2 minutes. Stir in the chiles and broth. Return meat and any accumulated juices to pot and let mixture come to a boil, then reduce heat, cover, and simmer until meat is tender, about 1½ hours. Remove from heat and let stand 5 to 10 minutes before serving, to settle flavors. To serve, garnish each portion with the additional cilantro leaves and a lime wedge.

In Chinese restaurants in San Francisco, there's nothing more soothing on a foggy night than a steaming bowl of braised greens with pork. This is a homespun version of that tonic. [SERVES 4]

ginger-braised spareribs with mustard greens

2 pounds baby back ribs

2 tablespoons vegetable oil

1 yellow onion, sliced

Kosher salt

3 garlic cloves

1 tablespoon minced fresh ginger

½ teaspoon red pepper flakes

12 ounces mustard greens, chopped

2 cups hot cooked brown or white rice

Kat Daddy's Pepper Vinegar (page 132) or rice vinegar

Have your butcher saw the ribs in half so that you have 2 sets of short riblets. At home, cut between bones to separate ribs. Rinse ribs and pat dry with paper towels.

Warm the oil in a 5- to 7-quart Dutch oven over medium-high heat. Place ribs in pot, meat sides down. Scatter the onion over ribs and sprinkle with salt. Let cook until ribs release from pot when prodded with a wooden spoon, about 5 minutes. At that point, stir ribs and onions and cook, stirring, a few minutes more until both take on a little color, about 3 minutes. Pour in 4 cups water. Smash the garlic with the side of a chef's knife and remove peel; add smashed garlic to pan. Bring mixture to a boil, reduce heat, cover, and simmer until rib meat is slipping from bones, about 1½ hours.

Stir in the ginger and red pepper flakes. Add the greens and stir until wilted. Cover pan again and cook until greens are tender, about 15 minutes. Spoon the rice into bowls, ladle ribs, greens, and broth on top, season to taste with vinegar, and serve.

A friend in Italy often serves me sausages and lentils when I visit. It's a traditional dish where she lives and is often prepared with stumpy *cotechino*; here I use good-quality Italian sausage. Umbrian lentils (*lenticchie*) are delicious and meaty if you can find them at an Italian market; or use green lentils du Puy or good old brown soup lentils. This is a humble dish, so the ingredients don't have to be pedigreed. [SERVES 4]

braised sausages with lentils

Olive oil

4 mild Italian sausages, about 12 ounces total

1 yellow onion, chopped

2 carrots, sliced

1 pound white or brown (cremini) mushrooms, cleaned

Kosher salt

1 cup dried lentils

¼ cup tomato paste

1 bay leaf

Freshly ground pepper

Chopped fresh Italian parsley leaves (optional)

Coat the bottom of a wide sauté pan with a thin film of the oil and set pan over medium-high heat. Prick the sausages a few times all over with a knife tip, then add to pan; shake pan to coat sausages with oil. Cover pan to keep fat from splattering and cook sausages, shaking pan occasionally (or turning the sausages with tongs as needed), until golden and slightly crispy all over, 4 to 5 minutes. Transfer sausages to a plate.

Put the onion and carrots in pan and cook until softened, stirring as needed. While vegetables are cooking, trim stems off the mushrooms and cut each mushroom into quarters; add mushrooms to pan, sprinkle well with salt, and cover pan. Let mushrooms cook until they give off a fair amount of liquid, about 5 minutes.

Stir in 2 cups water, the lentils, tomato paste, bay leaf, and a generous grinding of pepper; let come to a boil. Tuck sausages into lentils, then reduce heat, cover, and simmer until sausages are cooked through, about 25 minutes. Transfer sausages back to plate. Stir lentil mixture; if it seems dry, add another ½ cup water. Cover pan again and cook until lentils are tender, 15 to 20 minutes more.

When lentils are done, turn off heat. Slice sausages and stir into lentils; let stand for about 5 minutes to rewarm sausages, then serve, sprinkled with parsley, if desired.

If you find fava beans at the spring market, stir in a cup of those at the point when you let the stew stand (see page 113 for instructions on how to prepare beans). [SERVES 6]

spring lamb stew with artichokes and leeks

1 lemon

1 cup loosely packed fresh Italian parsley leaves, plus additional for garnish (optional)

3 cloves garlic

2 large leeks

3 pounds boneless lamb stew (from shoulder), trimmed of excess fat

Kosher salt

Freshly ground pepper

Olive oil

1 yellow onion, thinly sliced

¾ teaspoon dried thyme leaves

1½ cups chicken broth

12 small or "baby" artichokes

Pare zest from the lemon then set lemon aside. In a food processor or by hand, mince together zest, the 1 cup parsley leaves, and garlic. Trim the root end and green tops off the leeks. Slice white parts in half lengthwise, rinse layers well under running water, then slice thinly crosswise.

Cut the meat into 1-inch pieces, rinse, and pat dry. Sprinkle with salt and several grindings of pepper. Coat the bottom of a 5- to 7-quart Dutch oven with a thin film of the oil and set pot over medium-high heat. When oil shimmers, add enough meat to cover bottom in 1 layer. Cook, without stirring, until meat lifts easily from pot and is well browned on bottom, about 5 minutes. Turn and brown on the other side, 5 minutes more. Transfer to a plate and continue with remaining meat, adding more oil to pot in between batches as needed.

When last batch of meat has been removed, add leeks and the onion to pot and cook, stirring, until softened, about 5 minutes. Stir in parsley-lemon mixture and the thyme and cook until fragrant, about 30 seconds. Pour in the broth, stirring to release browned bits. Return meat and any accumulated juices to pot, let liquid come to a boil, then reduce heat, cover, and simmer until meat is tender when pierced, about 1½ hours.

Meanwhile, fill a bowl with water and squeeze reserved lemon into it; then drop it in. Working with 1 small artichoke at a time, tear off the dark green leaves to reach the tender yellow leaves. With a small sharp knife, pare away any tough green patches of leaf from the bottom, then trim off sharp tips. Cut each artichoke in half and drop into bowl of lemon water, to prevent discoloring. When meat is tender, drain artichokes (discard lemon) and add to pot. Let liquid come to a boil, then reduce heat, cover, and simmer until artichokes are cooked through, about 15 minutes. Remove from heat and let stand 5 to 10 minutes before serving, to settle flavors. Garnish with additional chopped parsley, if desired.

Lamb shanks are one of the great slow-cooked dishes—the longer they braise, the better they become. But browning the shanks on the stove (not to mention finding a pot big enough to hold more than two or three) is difficult. So I brown them in the oven in a heavy metal roasting pan that can also go on top of the burners, then tightly seal it for braising. [S E R V E S 6]

oven-braised lamb shanks with white beans

6 lamb shanks

Olive oil

1½ tablespoons Lemon-Rosemary Salt (page 133)

3 large yellow onions

1½ cups dried white beans, soaked overnight

Kosher salt

1½ cups dry white wine, such as Sauvignon Blanc

2 teaspoons dried thyme leaves

1 large can (28 ounces) chopped tomatoes

Preheat an oven to 450 degrees F.

Rinse the lamb shanks and pat dry with paper towels. Put in a large bowl and drizzle with enough of the oil to coat them, then sprinkle with the lemon-rosemary salt. Using your hands, toss shanks to distribute oil and salt. Spread shanks in a large, heavy roasting pan and place on the bottom rack of the oven. Roast, turning once or twice with tongs, until sizzling and lightly browned, 15 to 20 minutes. Meanwhile, slice 2 of the onions and set aside.

While shanks are browning, drain the soaked beans, put them in a saucepan, and add cold water to 3 inches above the beans. Peel the remaining onion, cut it in half (keep root end intact), and drop into pan. Bring beans to a boil over high heat, then reduce heat and simmer, uncovered, until beans are just tender, about 1 hour. Season well with kosher salt when cooked.

When shanks have browned, transfer roasting pan to the stove top, straddling 2 burners. Turn oven temperature down to 325 degrees F. Pour the wine into the roasting pan, scatter sliced onions and thyme over all, then add the tomatoes and 1 cup water. Turn burners under the roasting pan to medium-high and cook, stirring to release browned bits, until liquid comes to a boil. Turn off heat and cover roasting pan tightly with 2 layers of heavy-duty foil, place a baking sheet over pan to create a tight seal, then return pan to oven for 1 hour.

Drain beans, discarding onion. Remove shanks from oven and peel back foil; stir in beans. Re-cover pan with foil and baking sheet and return to oven. Cook until meat peels away from bone easily when prodded with a fork and beans are very tender, about 2½ hours longer, checking pan and stirring ingredients once or twice (if pan appears dry, add water as necessary). Remove pan from oven and let stand for 10 to 15 minutes before serving, to settle flavors.

Anyone who appreciates braising should experience a luscious tagine, the North African dish of slow-cooked meat or poultry and spices. Preserved Lemons (page 135) are the quintessential condiment and must be made weeks in advance, but they are simple to prepare. You can also buy them in some specialty markets. Serve this tagine with Apricot Couscous (page 116) and sliced fennel, mint, and radishes dressed with olive oil and lemon juice. [SERVES 6]

moroccan lamb tagine with preserved lemons

3 pounds boneless lamb stew
    (from shoulder), trimmed of excess fat
1 teaspoon ground cumin
1 teaspoon ground ginger
½ teaspoon ground cinnamon
Pinch saffron threads
1 orange
Leaves from ½ bunch fresh cilantro
3 garlic cloves
1 teaspoon kosher salt
2 yellow onions, finely chopped
1 can (14½ ounces) chopped tomatoes
1 cup pitted green Moroccan (or other)
    olives, chopped
Minced peel of 1 Preserved Lemon
    (optional)

Cut the meat into 1-inch pieces, rinse, and pat dry with paper towels. Place meat in a large bowl. In a small bowl, mix the cumin, ginger, cinnamon, and saffron; sprinkle over meat, then set aside.

Pare the zest from the orange, then juice the fruit; set juice aside. In a food processor or by hand, mince together the zest, cilantro, garlic, and salt until you have a paste. Add to meat along with orange juice and stir well to blend. Cover bowl and let stand at room temperature for 2 hours or overnight in the refrigerator.

Transfer mixture to a 5- to 7-quart Dutch oven and add the onions, tomatoes, and 1 cup water. Place pot over high heat and let come to a boil, then reduce heat, cover, and simmer until meat is tender, about 1½ hours. Add the olives, turn off heat, and let stand, covered, for 10 minutes for olives to heat through and flavors to settle. Sprinkle each serving with preserved lemon, if using.

In Italy, pasta ribbons are often topped with a wild boar sauce that's essentially a meaty, earthy stew. You can make a close facsimile with pork or with lamb (if you like a gamier taste), or a combination of the two. For another layer of flavor, serve over Herbed Wide Noodles (page 121) instead of pappardelle or garnish with Basil Gremolata (page 134). [SERVES 6]

pappardelle with ragù

2 pounds boneless lamb stew or pork stew (from shoulder) or 1 pound each, trimmed of excess fat

Kosher salt

Olive oil

4 ounces pancetta, diced

1 yellow onion, finely chopped

2 carrots, finely chopped

2 celery stalks, finely chopped

2 garlic cloves, minced

½ cup red wine

1 teaspoon paprika

1 large can (28 ounces) chopped tomatoes plus 1 can (14½ ounces) chopped tomatoes

1 bay leaf

1 pound pappardelle pasta or wide egg noodles

⅓ cup chopped fresh Italian parsley leaves

Coarsely grated Parmigiano-Reggiano or pecorino Romano cheese

Cut the meat into 1-inch pieces, rinse, and pat dry with paper towels. Sprinkle with salt. Coat the bottom of a 5- to 7-quart Dutch oven with a thin film of the oil and set pot over medium-high heat. When oil shimmers, add enough meat to cover bottom in 1 layer. Cook, without stirring, until meat lifts easily from pot with tongs and is well browned on bottom, about 5 minutes. Turn and brown on the other side, about 5 minutes more. Transfer meat to a plate and continue with remaining meat, adding more oil to pot in between batches as needed.

When last batch of meat has been removed, drain off all but about 1 table-spoon fat from pot. Add the pancetta and cook, stirring, until it renders most of its fat, about 1 minute. Add the onion, carrots, and celery. Cook, stirring often, until vegetables are softened, about 5 minutes. Add the garlic and cook for 1 minute. Pour in the wine and cook for 1 minute, stirring to release browned bits. Return meat and any accumulated juices to pot and stir in the paprika. Add the tomatoes and bay leaf and let come to a boil. Reduce heat, cover, and simmer until meat falls into shreds when pushed with the side of a spoon, about 2½ hours, stirring occasionally. Turn off heat and let stand while you cook the pasta.

Bring a large pot of salted water to a boil and add pappardelle; cook according to package directions until al dente. Drain pappardelle and divide among pasta bowls. Stir the parsley into ragù, ladle over pasta, sprinkle with cheese, and serve.

Meatballs have made a roaring comeback. A chic restaurant in my neighborhood even hosts a "meatball madness" night on Mondays. They are so simple to braise at home, why not have them any night? [SERVES 4 TO 6]

greek lamb meatballs

1½ pounds ground lamb

1 cup soft (fresh) breadcrumbs

2 large eggs

¼ cup finely chopped fresh mint leaves

¼ cup finely chopped fresh Italian parsley leaves

2 garlic cloves, minced

2 tablespoons Worcestershire sauce

1 teaspoon kosher salt

Pinch cayenne pepper

Olive oil

½ cup white wine

2 cans (14½ ounces each) chopped tomatoes

Put the meat into a large bowl and add the breadcrumbs, eggs, herbs, garlic, Worcestershire sauce, salt, and cayenne. With your hands, blend the mixture very well (at first it will seem wet; keep working until no longer moist). Shape meat into 2-inch meatballs, placing them on a platter as you work. Cover the meatballs with waxed or parchment paper and refrigerate for 30 minutes.

Choose a sauté pan or frying pan large enough to comfortably hold all the meatballs in 1 layer (or use 2 smaller pans) and coat the bottom with a thin film of the oil. Set pan over medium-high heat and when oil shimmers, add meatballs in 1 layer. Cook, without stirring, until meatballs lift easily from pan with tongs and are well browned on bottom, 3 to 5 minutes. Turn meatballs over and cook until browned on the other side, about 3 minutes more. Drain off fat (if using a large pan, it may be easier to remove fat with a bulb baster).

Pour in the wine and shake pan vigorously to release meatballs and any browned bits. Add the tomatoes and shake pan again, then let come to a boil. Reduce heat, cover, and simmer until meatballs are cooked through and tomatoes have thickened, 15 to 20 minutes. Turn off heat and let stand 5 minutes before serving, to settle flavors.

This is the poorest of recipes with the richest of results. Halfway between a soup and a stew, I crave bowlfuls of it when I am run down—it's healthy, restorative, and mindless to make. And I'm not shy about using a bouillon cube for the broth when that's all I have on hand. [SERVES 4]

southern-style greens with ham

1½ pounds dandelion greens

12 ounces ham steak

2 medium leeks

3 tablespoons olive oil

2 cups chicken or vegetable broth

Freshly ground pepper

4 cups hot cooked brown or white rice

Kat Daddy's Pepper Vinegar (page 132) or rice vinegar

Trim ends off the dandelion stems, then chop stems and leaves coarsely. Rinse greens, shake in a colander to rid of excess moisture, and set aside. Dice the ham, discarding fat and center bone if there is one. Trim the root end and green tops off the leeks. Slice white parts in half lengthwise, rinse layers well under running water, then slice thinly crosswise.

In a 3- to 4-quart saucepan, warm the oil over medium-high heat until it shimmers. Add leeks and ham and cook, stirring, until leeks are softened, about 4 minutes. Pour in the broth and let come to a boil. Add dandelion greens and stems by the handful, stirring each addition until it wilts down. Season well with pepper, reduce heat to medium, cover, and cook until greens are very tender and almost slippery, about 40 minutes. Spoon the rice into bowls and ladle greens, broth, and ham over rice. Season to taste with vinegar and serve.

Chapter 3
POULTRY

A chicken in every pot may have been a recipe to heal a nation once, but it's also given us some of the world's best recipes—chicken curry, coq au vin, and pot pie to name just a few. Chickens are ideal for braising because of their size and structure; one cut-up chicken fits perfectly in a Dutch oven and feeds a family. The bones give the sauce body and flavor and keep the meat from drying out. With all poultry, dark meat is the best for slow-cooking. Chicken thighs cook up moist and succulent, but don't braise a boneless chicken breast; it just toughens. Turkey legs are inexpensive gems for the pot and even small birds such as poussin and game hens work, especially if you like the idea of eating right off the bone. Poultry's mild taste is a canvas for any flavor, from spicy to creamy to garlicky. No wonder it's found on dinner tables around the world.

Coq au vin is traditionally made with red wine, but I've never liked the color of that dish. So I use Sauvignon Blanc, but you can use any dry white wine that you might have in the fridge. I also braise this without a lid so that the chicken skin stays crisper and the sauce fully concentrates. Serve with Herbed Wide Noodles (page 121) and spinach sautéed in olive oil. [SERVES 4]

white wine coq au vin

1 roasting chicken (4 to 5 pounds), cut up, legs split into drumsticks and thighs, and breasts halved crosswise

Kosher salt

Olive oil

2 strips thick (butcher) bacon

8 ounces regular white or brown (cremini) mushrooms, cleaned

1 yellow onion, thinly sliced

2 carrots, diced

About 1½ cups chicken broth

½ teaspoon dried thyme leaves

1 cup dry white wine, such as Sauvignon Blanc

12 small white or red potatoes, quartered

Freshly ground pepper

Minced fresh Italian parsley leaves

Preheat an oven to 350 degrees F.

Rinse the chicken and pat dry with paper towels. Sprinkle with salt. Coat the bottom of a 12-inch sauté pan or a 5- to 7-quart Dutch oven with a thin film of the oil and set over medium-high heat. When oil shimmers, add chicken, skin sides down, without crowding; do in batches if necessary. Cook until skin is golden brown and chicken releases easily from pan when lifted with tongs, about 5 minutes. Turn pieces over and cook until they brown and release easily on the other side, about 5 minutes more. Transfer browned chicken to a plate.

Meanwhile, slice the bacon strips in half lengthwise, then slice crosswise into small pieces. Cut the mushrooms into halves, if small, or into quarters, if large.

When last batch of chicken has been removed, add bacon to pan and cook, stirring, until fat is rendered. Drain off all but about 2 tablespoons of fat, then add the onion and carrots and cook, stirring often, until vegetables are softened, about 3 minutes. Add mushrooms, then stir in ½ cup of the broth and the thyme, stirring to release browned bits. Let come to a boil, then reduce heat, cover, and simmer until mushrooms have cooked down by half, about 7 minutes.

Pour in the wine and let come to a boil; stir in the potatoes and season with salt and pepper. Tuck chicken pieces into pan in 1 layer. Pour in enough remaining broth to come halfway up sides of chicken. Let liquid come to a boil, then transfer pan, uncovered, to the oven and cook until potatoes are tender and chicken is opaque at the bone, about 45 minutes, basting chicken a few times with pan juices. Sprinkle with parsley and serve.

I learned of chicken bouillabaisse—a simple braise of chicken in saffron broth—from Judy Rodgers's incredible *Zuni Café Cookbook* and have expanded the idea with a blend of garlicky beans stirred in to give it a pan-Mediterranean mood. Serve with toasted baguette slices. [SERVES 6]

chicken bouillabaisse with garlicky beans

6 chicken legs, split into drumsticks and thighs, skinned

Kosher salt

6 tablespoons olive oil

1 yellow onion, sliced

½ cup dry white wine, such as Sauvignon Blanc

4-inch strip orange zest

1 teaspoon dried thyme leaves

Generous pinch saffron threads

1 can (14½ ounces) chopped tomatoes

1 cup chicken broth

2 cans (15 ounces each) garbanzo beans, drained and rinsed

2 garlic cloves, minced

¾ teaspoon red pepper flakes

½ cup chopped fresh mint leaves

4 ounces crumbled feta cheese

Freshly ground pepper

Preheat an oven to 375 degrees F.

Rinse the chicken and pat dry with paper towels. Sprinkle with salt. Heat 3 tablespoons of the oil in a 5- to 7-quart Dutch oven over medium-high heat; add the onion, sprinkle with salt to taste, and cook, stirring, until softened, about 3 minutes. Add the wine, zest, thyme, and saffron and let come to a boil. Add the tomatoes and broth and bring to a boil again. Put chicken in pot, pushing it down into the sauce. Cover and transfer to the oven. Cook until chicken is opaque at the bone, about 45 minutes.

Meanwhile, in a baking dish, stir together the beans, remaining 3 tablespoons oil, garlic, and red pepper flakes. Put in oven alongside the chicken for the last 15 minutes of cooking time. Remove beans from oven and stir in the mint and feta; season with salt and pepper. Spoon beans into bowls and top with chicken and sauce.

During a chat about farmers' markets with famed chef Alice Waters, I learned an invaluable lesson: Go in winter, when the farmers need you most. There's a double reason, too, if you are braising, because that's when sturdy root vegetables are spilling out of the bins. Serve this with Golden Pilaf (page 118) and top with Yogurt-Mint Sauce (page 131). [SERVES 6 TO 8]

winter market chicken

6 chicken legs, split into drumsticks
   and thighs
1/3 cup freshly squeezed lime juice
3 garlic cloves
Vegetable oil
Kosher salt
1 small yellow onion, chopped
2-inch piece fresh ginger, peeled
1 serrano or jalapeño chile pepper,
   stemmed and seeded
1 tablespoon ground cumin
2 teaspoons ground coriander
1 teaspoon turmeric
2 turnips (about 6 ounces total)
1 yam or sweet potato (about 10 ounces)
6 small white rose, Yukon gold, or red
   new potatoes
2 carrots
1 cup chicken broth
1 can (14½ ounces) chopped tomatoes

Rinse the chicken and pat dry with paper towels. Put in a bowl and pour the lime juice over chicken, press 1 garlic clove into bowl, add 1 tablespoon oil and 1 teaspoon salt, and mix well. Let chicken marinate, covered, at room temperature for 1 hour.

Meanwhile, in a food processor or by hand, mince the onion, ginger, chile, and remaining 2 garlic cloves. In a small bowl, stir together the cumin, coriander, and turmeric. Peel the turnips and yam and cut into 1-inch cubes; scrub the potatoes and cut into quarters; scrub carrots and cut into 1-inch lengths. Set ingredients aside.

Coat the bottom of an 8-to 10-quart Dutch oven with a thin film of oil and set over medium-high heat. When oil shimmers, lift chicken from marinade with tongs (reserve marinade in bowl), shaking off excess, and put in pot, skin sides down, without crowding (be careful of hot oil spitting from marinade); do in batches if necessary. Cook until skin is golden brown and chicken releases easily from pot when lifted with tongs, about 5 minutes. Turn pieces over and cook until they brown and release easily on the other side, about 5 minutes more. Transfer browned chicken to a plate.

When last batch of chicken has been removed, add onion mixture to pot and cook, stirring, for about 1 minute, until fragrant. Stir in cumin mixture and cook for 30 seconds, until fragrant. Pour in the broth and reserved marinade in bowl, stirring to release browned bits, then add the tomatoes. Let mixture come to a boil, then stir in turnips, yam, potatoes, and carrots. Let return to a boil, then tuck reserved chicken and any accumulated juices into pot. Reduce heat, cover, and simmer until root vegetables are tender and chicken is almost falling off the bone, about 1½ hours.

Escarole is the queen of chicories in my opinion, although her sisters—curly endive (or frisée), radicchio, and Treviso—can be used in this dish. Slow-simmering the greens with aromatics and juices from the chicken turns them indescribably tender and sweet. The piquancy of lemons and olives offsets that. Serve this with slices of toasted, garlic-rubbed bread or with Shortcut Risotto (page 123). [SERVES 4]

chicken with escarole, lemon, and olives

1 roasting chicken (4 to 5 pounds), cut up, legs split into drumsticks and thighs, and breasts halved crosswise

Kosher salt

Olive oil

8 whole shallots

6 garlic cloves

½ cup dry white wine

1 head escarole, core trimmed and leaves coarsely chopped

1 lemon, very thinly sliced, seeds removed

1 cup black oil-cured olives (with pits) or pitted kalamata olives

Rinse the chicken and pat dry with paper towels. Sprinkle with salt. Coat the bottom of a 5- to 7-quart Dutch oven with a thin film of the oil and set over medium-high heat. When oil shimmers, add chicken, skin sides down, without crowding; do in batches if necessary. Cook until skin is golden brown and chicken pieces release easily from pot when lifted with tongs, about 5 minutes. Turn pieces over and cook until they are brown and release easily on the other side, about 5 minutes more. Transfer browned chicken to a plate.

While chicken is browning, peel the shallots and trim off root ends. Peel the garlic.

When last batch of chicken has been removed, put shallots and garlic in pot and stir for about 30 seconds until fragrant; sprinkle with a little salt. Pour in the wine, stirring to release browned bits. Shake pot to spread out shallots and garlic. Add the escarole, but do not stir. Cover pot and let escarole wilt, about 5 minutes. Arrange the lemon slices in 1 layer over escarole; do not stir. Sprinkle with a little salt. Arrange chicken, with any accumulated juices, on top of lemons; do not stir. Cover pot and reduce heat to medium-low. Cook until chicken is opaque at the bone, about 45 minutes. Turn off heat.

Scatter the olives over chicken and, with a large spoon, gently stir contents of pot. Cover pot again and let stand for about 10 minutes to warm olives, then divide chicken, vegetables, and olives among shallow pasta plates or bowls and spoon juices over.

Unlike most braises, this one is simmered uncovered so that the browned chicken skin stays crisper and the sauce condenses. Serve with Golden Pilaf (page 118) or brown rice. [SERVES 6]

spicy coconut-chicken curry

6 chicken legs, split into drumsticks
    and thighs
Kosher salt
Vegetable oil
1 yellow onion, sliced
2 garlic cloves, minced
1-inch piece fresh ginger, peeled
    and minced
3 tablespoons curry powder,
    preferably Madras
1 teaspoon ground cumin
½ teaspoon cayenne pepper
1 can (14½ ounces) chopped tomatoes,
    drained
About 1 can (15 ounces) light coconut milk
1 cup frozen, thawed peas
¼ cup chopped fresh cilantro leaves

Rinse the chicken and pat dry with paper towels. Sprinkle with salt. Coat the bottom of 5- to 7-quart Dutch oven with a thin film of the oil and set over medium-high heat. When oil shimmers, add chicken, skin sides down, without crowding; do in batches if necessary. Cook until skin is golden brown and chicken releases easily from pot when lifted with tongs, about 5 minutes. Turn pieces over and cook until they brown and release easily on the other side, about 5 minutes more. Transfer browned chicken to a plate.

When last batch of chicken has been removed, add the onion, garlic, and ginger to pot and cook, stirring, until vegetables are soft and fragrant, about 3 minutes. Add the curry powder, cumin, cayenne, and ½ teaspoon salt. Cook for 30 seconds until spices are fragrant, then stir in the tomatoes and 1 cup of the coconut milk. Stir well and let come to a boil. Return chicken and any accumulated juices to pot; chicken should be surrounded by sauce, but not submerged in it, so that topmost skin is exposed (if there is not enough liquid in pot, add remaining coconut milk from can). Reduce heat and simmer, uncovered, until chicken is opaque at the bone, about 45 minutes. Stir in the peas and cilantro and cook until peas are hot, about 5 minutes more.

For this dish, each element cooks down and braises in its own liquid to extract the essence. While we tend to use sage only at Thanksgiving, in central Italy, it is used with pork and chicken all the time. Herbed Wide Noodles (page 121), including some extra sage, are a particularly good base for those heavenly juices. [SERVES 6]

tuscan chicken stew

10 boneless, skinless chicken thighs

2 red bell peppers

1 yellow bell pepper

1 pound white or brown (cremini) mushrooms, cleaned

¼ cup extra-virgin olive oil

1 yellow onion, sliced

2 garlic cloves, minced

½ cup Marsala, Madeira, or dry sherry

Kosher salt

¼ cup finely chopped fresh sage leaves

Cut the chicken into 2-inch pieces; set aside. Cut the bell peppers into quarters and remove stems, seeds, and ribs. Thinly slice each quarter crosswise to make short strips. Trim stems off the mushrooms, then either cut mushrooms into quarters, if small, or eighths, if large. Set vegetables aside.

In a 5- to 7-quart Dutch oven over medium-high heat, warm the oil. When it shimmers, add the onion and cook, stirring occasionally, until onion starts to color, about 5 minutes. Stir in the garlic and bell peppers. Cover pot and cook, stirring once or twice, until peppers have softened, about 10 minutes. Add chicken. Cook, stirring a few times, until chicken is no longer pink, about 2 minutes. Pour in the Marsala and let come to a boil, then stir in a good pinch of salt. Fold in mushrooms, then cover pot, reduce heat to low, and let vegetables and chicken cook until tender and juicy, about 20 minutes. Stir in the sage and serve.

Sumptuous spices and fruit, plus a splash of exotic rose water, hint at the regal roots of this dish. I got the recipe from one of my favorite princesses of cuisine, Sara Whiteford. Serve with Apricot Couscous (page 116), deleting the dried apricots and stirring in toasted slivered almonds instead. [SERVES 4]

sara's persian chicken

8 bone-in chicken thighs, skinned

½ teaspoon ground cardamom

½ teaspoon ground cumin

½ teaspoon cinnamon

½ teaspoon kosher salt

Vegetable oil

1 yellow onion, chopped

2 garlic cloves, minced

1-inch piece fresh ginger, peeled and minced

Pinch saffron threads

Pinch cayenne pepper

½ cup freshly squeezed lime juice

¼ cup sugar

1 cup chicken broth

1 cup dried apricots

Rose water (optional)

Rinse the chicken and pat dry. In a small bowl, mix together the cardamom, cumin, cinnamon, and salt. Sprinkle half of spice mixture over chicken.

Coat the bottom of a 5- to 7-quart Dutch oven with a thin film of the oil and set pot over medium-high heat. When oil shimmers, add enough chicken to cover bottom in 1 layer. Cook, without stirring, until chicken lifts easily from pot with tongs and is browned on bottom, about 5 minutes. Turn pieces over and cook until they brown and release easily on the other side, about 5 minutes more. Transfer browned chicken to a plate.

When last batch of chicken has been removed, add the onion, garlic, and ginger to pot and cook, stirring, for 1 minute until fragrant. Stir in the saffron, cayenne, and remaining spice mixture. Add the lime juice and sugar and let come to a boil, stirring to release browned bits. Add the broth and return chicken and any accumulated juices to pot. Let liquid come to a boil, then reduce heat, cover, and simmer for 25 minutes. Meanwhile, cut each dried apricot in half crosswise.

When chicken has cooked 25 minutes, stir in apricots. Continue to simmer, covered, until chicken is opaque at the bone and apricots are plump, 10 to 15 minutes more. To serve, splash each portion with a few drops of rose water, if using.

Everyone seems to crave the simple flavors of this "hunter's stew," a homey Italian standard. Be sure to reduce the pot juices so that the sauce is thick enough to coat the chicken and whatever side dish you are serving, whether that be Herbed Wide Noodles (page 121) or new potatoes roasted with Lemon-Rosemary Salt (page 133) and olive oil. [SERVES 6]

chicken cacciatore

6 chicken legs, split into drumsticks and
    thighs
Kosher salt
½ teaspoon paprika
Olive oil
1 two-ounce slice prosciutto, about
    ⅛ inch thick
1 red or yellow onion, sliced
1 red bell pepper, chopped
½ cup dry white wine such as Pinot Grigio
    or dry vermouth
1 large can (28 ounces) chopped tomatoes

Rinse the chicken and pat dry with paper towels. Sprinkle with salt and the paprika. Coat the bottom of a 5- to 7-quart Dutch oven with a thin film of the oil and set over medium-high heat. When oil shimmers, add chicken, skin sides down, without crowding; do in batches if necessary. Cook until skin is golden brown and chicken releases easily from pot when lifted with tongs, about 5 minutes. Turn pieces over and cook until they brown and release easily on the other side, about 5 minutes more. Transfer browned chicken to a plate and continue with remaining meat as necessary, adding more oil to pot in between batches as needed.

Meanwhile, cut the prosciutto crosswise into thin strips, then cut strips crosswise again into dice.

When last batch of chicken is removed from pot, add prosciutto, the onion, and bell pepper, and cook, stirring occasionally, until vegetables are softened, about 3 minutes. Pour in the wine and cook, stirring to release browned bits, for 1 minute, then add the tomatoes. Let mixture come to a boil, then return chicken and any accumulated juices to pot. Turn chicken pieces with tongs to coat with sauce. Reduce heat, cover, and simmer until chicken is opaque at the bone, about 45 minutes. Transfer chicken pieces to a plate with tongs and tent with foil to keep warm. Bring sauce in pot to a boil and cook, stirring often, until thickened, about 10 minutes. Divide chicken pieces among plates, ladle sauce evenly over each portion, and serve.

Posole is the iconic Christmas dish in Santa Fe. There's no master recipe, but it always must contain hominy—lime-soaked corn—in either dried or canned form. The other must-have ingredient is ground dried chile, such as ancho or New Mexico, which is available in many grocery stores or in Latin American markets. Do not confuse it with chili powder, which contains other spices and herbs. [SERVES 4]

turkey posole

2 turkey drumsticks, about 2½ pounds total

Kosher salt

Vegetable oil

1 white onion, chopped

3 garlic cloves, thinly sliced

2 teaspoons ground chile
  (see recipe introduction)

1 teaspoon dried oregano leaves

2 cups chicken broth

1 can (15 ounces) golden hominy, drained
  and rinsed

Freshly ground pepper

Garnishes

1 lime, cut into wedges

¼ cup chopped fresh cilantro

2 green onions, sliced

1 small avocado, diced

1 cup finely chopped green cabbage

Rinse the turkey and pat dry with paper towels. Sprinkle with salt. Coat the bottom of a 5- to 7-quart Dutch oven with a thin film of the oil and set over medium-high heat. When oil shimmers, add turkey and cook until skin is golden and turkey releases easily from pan when lifted with tongs, about 5 minutes. Continue to cook, turning with tongs as necessary, until golden all over, 8 to 10 minutes more.

Leaving turkey in pot, add the onion, garlic, ground chile, and oregano. Pour in the broth and stir well to release browned bits. Let come to a boil, then reduce heat, cover, and simmer until meat is falling off the bone, about 1½ hours, turning turkey once or twice during cooking.

Transfer turkey with tongs to a plate and set aside. Turn off heat, tilt pot, and spoon off as much fat as possible. Stir in the hominy, cover, and let sit while turkey cools. (Or, if made ahead, do not defat mixture; stir in hominy. Let cool, cover, and refrigerate separately from turkey for up to 1 day. Lift off fat from hominy mixture and proceed with recipe.)

When turkey is cool enough to handle, pull off and discard skin, then pull meat off bone, shredding with your fingers as you work. Stir turkey meat into pot and bring mixture to a boil; reduce heat and simmer until turkey is heated through, about 5 minutes (or longer if chilled). Season with salt and pepper. Ladle into bowls and squeeze a lime wedge over each portion, then garnish with cilantro, green onions, avocado, and cabbage as desired.

Pot pie is essentially a creamy stew with pastry on top. For this streamlined version, turkey drumsticks are braised to flavor the sauce and the crust is baked separately so it doesn't get gummy underneath. Easy as (pot) pie. [SERVES 4]

turkey pot pie in a pan

2 turkey drumsticks, about 2½ pounds total

Kosher salt

Vegetable oil

4 fresh parsley sprigs

4 fresh thyme sprigs

1 bay leaf

1 yellow onion, chopped

2 celery stalks, chopped

1 large carrot, chopped

2½ cups chicken broth

1 large baking potato (about 10 ounces), peeled and diced

1 cup heavy cream

½ teaspoon dried thyme leaves

Pastry for a 9-inch pie, homemade or purchased

1 cup frozen, thawed peas

Freshly ground pepper

Rinse the turkey and pat dry with paper towels. Sprinkle with salt. Coat the bottom of a 10- to 12-inch-wide sauté pan or deep frying pan with a thin film of the oil and set over medium-high heat. When oil shimmers, add turkey and cook until skin is golden and turkey releases easily from pan when lifted with tongs, about 5 minutes. Continue to cook, turning with tongs as necessary, until golden all over, 8 to 10 minutes more.

While turkey is browning, put the parsley, thyme sprigs, and bay leaf in a piece of doubled cheesecloth and tie it to make a bouquet garni.

When turkey is browned, transfer to a plate and stir the onion, celery, and carrot into pan. Pour in the broth and tuck in bouquet garni; let come to a boil. Return turkey to pan, reduce heat, cover, and simmer until meat is starting to pull from the bone, about 1 hour. In the last 15 minutes or so, preheat an oven to 350 degrees F.

Transfer cooked turkey back to plate and set aside. Discard bouquet garni. Add the potatoes, cream, and thyme leaves to pan and let come to a boil. Reduce heat, cover, and simmer until potatoes are tender and cream is thickened, about 25 minutes, stirring occasionally.

Meanwhile, roll out or trim the pastry to ½ inch larger than the diameter of the turkey pan and place pastry circle on a baking sheet. Bake until golden brown, 20 to 25 minutes (it will shrink slightly). While pastry is baking, pull off and discard turkey skin, then cut meat off bone; chop meat into small pieces.

Add the peas and chopped turkey to reduced cream mixture in pan and heat through, about 5 minutes; season with salt and pepper. Remove from heat and set cooked pastry on top of mixture in pan. To serve, spoon out portions of turkey, sauce, and crust directly from pan.

Once little game hens or *poussins* (baby chickens) are braised, they are tender enough to pull apart with your hands, which works well since this sauce is positively lickable. This recipe is flexible: If you don't have fresh sage on hand, substitute dried thyme (dried sage has so little flavor); use saffron to add warm color, or not; or leave out the olives and cook some baby carrots with the birds instead. Serve game hens over Farrotto (page 119) or rice. [SERVES 4]

game hens in a pot

4 Cornish game hens or poussins
  (about 1 pound each)
Kosher salt
Olive oil
3 whole shallots, sliced
3 celery stalks, thinly sliced
2 ounces prosciutto, sliced about ¼ inch
  thick, then diced
2 tablespoons chopped fresh sage leaves or
  1 tablespoon dried thyme leaves
Pinch saffron threads (optional)
1½ cups chicken broth
½ cup pitted green olives (about 3 ounces)
Farrotto or cooked rice

Rinse the birds and pat dry with paper towels; sprinkle with salt. Coat the bottom of a 5- to 7-quart Dutch oven with a thin film of the oil and set over medium-high heat. When oil shimmers, add birds, breast sides down. Cook until skin is golden brown and birds release easily from pot when lifted with tongs, about 5 minutes. Turn over and cook until they brown and release easily on the other side, about 5 minutes more. Transfer browned birds to a plate.

Put the shallots, celery, and prosciutto in pot and cook, stirring, until just softened, about 3 minutes. Stir in the sage and saffron (if using). Pour in the broth and let come to a boil; arrange birds, breast sides up, in pot, fitting snugly. Reduce heat to low, cover, and simmer until legs of birds move very easily in sockets when wiggled, about 35 minutes. Carefully transfer birds back to plate with tongs. Stir the olives into pot and let cook until warmed through, about 3 minutes. Meanwhile, if desired, pull or cut out backbones from birds and cut birds in half for easier serving, or serve birds whole. Divide farrotto or rice among shallow bowls, top with birds, and ladle sauce over all.

Chapter 4

FISH AND SHELLFISH

Don't pass up the fish counter when you are thinking about braising. Even though seafood is more delicate than meat or poultry, the same exchange of flavors that makes those dishes so irresistible applies to fish and shellfish. Scallops are the perfect example: They are meaty and firm and can be browned, deglazed, and simmered, but it's a matter of minutes rather than hours so you can get a seafood stew on the table even at the end of a busy day. Many of the great seafaring cultures have iconic braised dishes. The bouillabaisse of Marseilles is probably the most famous (and the one in this chapter is easy to make), but there's Sicily's swordfish stew with capers, Thailand's fish curry, and Portugal's clever match of clams with sausage. Ask your fishmonger to guide you to the best of the local catch—halibut, wild salmon, monkfish, and shrimp are among the choices that make light, quick, unforgettable braises.

True bouillabaisse is an all-day affair to make; this rendition retains the classic fennel, leek, and saffron flavors, and the *rouille*, or spicy mayonnaise garnish, but takes far less time. For the bouquet garni, pare off strips of the orange zest with a vegetable peeler. [SERVES 4]

shortcut bouillabaisse

1 medium leek
1 fennel bulb
4 fresh thyme sprigs
2 strips orange zest
3 tablespoons olive oil
¼ teaspoon saffron threads
½ cup dry white wine
3 cups vegetable broth or chicken broth
1½ pounds halibut, cod, or rockfish fillets, cut into 1-inch pieces
8 diagonal slices baguette, about ¼ inch thick
¼ cup mayonnaise
1 garlic clove, pressed
Pinch cayenne pepper

Cut root end and green tops off the leek. Slice white part of leek in half lengthwise, then rinse layers well. Slice leek thinly crosswise. Cut green tops off the fennel bulb, cut it in half lengthwise, cut out the core, then slice each half thinly crosswise, reserving about ¼ cup of the feathery leaves. Put the thyme, zest, and reserved fennel leaves in a piece of doubled cheesecloth and tie it to make a bouquet garni.

Heat 2 tablespoons of the oil in a 10- to 12-inch-wide sauté pan or frying pan over medium-high heat and add leek and fennel slices; cook, stirring, until softened, about 5 minutes. Crumble in the saffron and pour in the wine, letting it boil for about 1 minute. Add the broth and let come to a boil. Add the bouquet garni, reduce heat, cover, and simmer 45 minutes. Place the fish in pan, cover again, and cook until fish is opaque, about 5 minutes.

Meanwhile, place the bread on a baking sheet and toast in the broiler until golden on both sides; brush with remaining oil. In a small bowl, stir together the mayonnaise, garlic, and cayenne. Ladle bouillabaisse into shallow bowls and top with a spoonful of spiced mayonnaise; angle 2 slices of toasted bread in each bowl and serve.

I adore this dish, with its mosaic of diced zucchini, potatoes, and tiny red tomatoes surrounding white fish. Timing is crucial, so be sure to prep all the ingredients ahead of time. Substitute monkfish for the halibut when it's available. [SERVES 4]

summer stew with halibut

2 tablespoons butter

2 tablespoons olive oil

2 green onions, sliced

2 medium red potatoes (about 8 ounces total), cut into ½-inch dice

1¼ cups vegetable broth or chicken broth

½ teaspoon fresh or ¼ teaspoon dried thyme leaves

Kosher salt

4 skinless pieces halibut or monkfish (about 6 ounces each)

1 cup tiny red cherry tomatoes, such as Sweet 100s, stemmed

1 medium zucchini (about 4 ounces), cut into ½-inch dice

1 cup fresh corn kernels (about 1 cob)

1 lemon, juiced

In a 10- to 12-inch-wide sauté pan or frying pan over medium heat, melt 1 tablespoon of the butter in 1 tablespoon of the oil. Add the onions and cook, stirring, for 1 minute. Add the potatoes and cook, stirring to coat with butter and oil, for 1 minute. Pour in 1 cup of the broth then add the thyme and a pinch of salt. Let come to a boil, then reduce heat, cover, and simmer 10 minutes.

Meanwhile, rinse the fish and pat dry with paper towels.

Stir the tomatoes, zucchini, and corn into pan, then cover again and continue to cook while you prepare the fish: In a wide nonstick skillet over medium-high heat, melt remaining butter in remaining oil. When foam subsides, add fish and cook until it is lightly golden on bottom and releases easily from skillet with tongs, about 3 minutes. Turn fish over and cook until it releases on other side, about 2 minutes (slightly longer if using monkfish). Immediately transfer fish to pan with vegetables, then pour remaining broth into skillet, stirring to release browned bits. Pour contents of skillet into pan with vegetables and fish, then cover pan and continue cooking until fish is barely translucent in center and potatoes are tender, about 4 minutes for halibut, 6 minutes for monkfish. Stir the lemon juice into pan, then divide fish among shallow bowls and spoon vegetables and sauce around fish.

When May turns to June, most people start craving summer vacation, but I start craving wild King salmon and peas, both at peak season. Why not pair this rich fish with a little cream and share it with a favorite companion? It's one of those recipes that's ideal for two. [SERVES 2]

salmon ragout with tarragon

2 plum (Roma) tomatoes

1 medium leek

2 tablespoons butter

Kosher salt

⅓ cup dry white wine or vermouth

¾ cup vegetable broth or chicken broth

2 tablespoons chopped fresh tarragon leaves, plus extra leaves for garnish

1 pound peas in the pod, shelled (about 1 cup) or 1 cup frozen, unthawed peas

12 ounces skinless salmon fillet

¼ cup heavy cream

8 small red new potatoes, cooked and quartered

Cut the tomatoes in half lengthwise and gently squeeze out seed sacs; dice tomatoes. Set aside.

Cut root end and green tops off the leek. Slice white part in half lengthwise, then rinse layers well. Slice leek thinly crosswise. Melt the butter in an 8- to 9-inch-wide sauté pan over medium-high heat and add leek; sprinkle with salt. Cook, stirring often, until leek is very soft, about 5 minutes. Pour in the wine and cook until almost evaporated, about 1 minute. Add the tomatoes, broth, and tarragon and bring to a boil. Stir in the peas, reduce heat to medium, and simmer, uncovered, until peas are just tender, 5 to 8 minutes.

Meanwhile, rinse the salmon and pat dry with paper towels. Cut fish crosswise into strips about 2 inches wide, then cut strips into 2-inch pieces.

When peas are tender, stir the cream into pan and let come to a boil. Place salmon in pan and reduce heat to medium, cover, and cook until salmon is still slightly pink in center, about 5 minutes. Divide the cooked potatoes between 2 shallow bowls, ladle salmon ragout over, and garnish with extra tarragon leaves.

This ancient dish is made with Sicily's most famous ingredients: olives, capers, tomatoes, pine nuts, and of course, swordfish. Traditionally, the stew includes sultanas (golden raisins) for a sweet-sour contrast, but I prefer piney rosemary. To toast pine nuts, shake them in a small frying pan over medium-high heat for a few minutes until lightly browned. [SERVES 4]

sicilian swordfish stew

2 pounds swordfish steaks, skin removed

¼ cup olive oil

1 small yellow onion, chopped

2 garlic cloves, coarsely chopped

¼ cup dry white wine, such as Pinot Grigio

1½ teaspoons minced fresh rosemary leaves

2 medium ripe red tomatoes (about 12 ounces total), seeded and chopped

¾ cup pitted green olives

¼ cup capers, rinsed

¼ cup toasted pine nuts

Kosher salt

Cut the swordfish into 1-inch strips, then cut into 1-inch pieces. Set aside.

In a 10- to 12-inch-wide sauté pan or frying pan, warm the oil over medium-high heat. Stir in the onion and cook, stirring often, until it starts to color, about 5 minutes. Stir in the garlic and cook for 30 seconds. Stir in the wine and rosemary and let come to a boil. Add the swordfish, tomatoes, olives, and capers and let come to a boil, stirring gently. Reduce heat, cover, and simmer until fish is opaque and tomatoes have broken down, about 8 minutes. Stir in the pine nuts, season with salt, and serve.

Making a Thai-style dish at home requires a few special ingredients; fortunately, most of them can be found at supermarkets. Look for lemongrass in the produce section, and fish sauce, curry paste, and canned coconut milk in the Asian or International section (Thai Kitchen is a very reliable brand). If you can't find Thai or purple basil, use regular basil. Serve curry with steamed jasmine rice. [SERVES 4 TO 6]

thai fish and corn curry

1 pound skinless halibut fillets, other firm
    white fish fillets, or bay scallops
1 stalk lemongrass
½ bunch fresh cilantro
2-inch piece fresh ginger
1 whole shallot
2 limes, juiced
3 tablespoons fish sauce
2 teaspoons brown sugar
2 tablespoons vegetable oil
¾ cup vegetable broth or chicken broth
2 cups (2 cobs) fresh or frozen, unthawed
    corn kernels
1 teaspoon green curry paste
½ cup coconut milk
1 cup fresh Thai basil leaves, torn into
    pieces

Rinse the fish and pat dry with paper towels. Cut fish into 1-inch pieces (if using bay scallops, just rinse and pat dry). Set fish aside.

Peel tough outer leaves off the lemongrass, then trim 3 inches from tender bottom end of stalk. Chop this piece and put in a food processor. Trim root ends off the cilantro, then cut about 2 inches of stems off leaves and add to food processor; set cilantro leaves aside. Peel the ginger and cut into pieces; add to food processor. Peel the shallot and add to food processor. Whirl lemongrass, cilantro stems, ginger, and shallot in processor until finely minced. In a small bowl, stir together the lime juice, fish sauce, and sugar. Set ingredients aside.

In a 3- to 4-quart saucepan, warm the oil over medium-high heat and add lemongrass mixture from food processor; cook, stirring, until fragrant, about 1 minute. Stir in the broth and corn. Reduce heat, cover, and simmer until corn is just tender, about 10 minutes. Stir in the curry paste, then the coconut milk and lime juice mixture and let come to a boil. Stir in fish or scallops, reduce heat, cover, and simmer until fish is cooked through, about 5 minutes. Remove from heat, stir in the basil and a handful of reserved cilantro leaves, and serve.

This is one of my favorite throw-together dinners, especially when I see plump rock shrimp (which usually have not been previously frozen like other shrimp) in the market. It's composed so that each layer absorbs the essence of the one before it, building deep flavor despite the simple preparation. Serve with Golden Pilaf (page 118) or small pasta, such as orzo.

[SERVES 4]

greek shrimp with zucchini and feta

2 tablespoons olive oil

1 whole shallot, thinly sliced

1 garlic clove, minced

2 teaspoons fresh or 1 teaspoon dried oregano leaves

3 medium zucchini (about 12 ounces total), sliced ¼ inch thick

Kosher salt

3 medium ripe tomatoes (about 1¼ pounds), peeled, seeded, and chopped, or 1 can (14½ ounces) chopped tomatoes, drained

1 pound peeled, deveined rock shrimp or medium prawns

⅓ cup crumbled feta cheese

Warm the oil in a 10- to 12-inch-wide sauté pan over medium-high heat. Add the shallot and garlic and stir until fragrant, about 1 minute. Sprinkle with the oregano and stir for a few seconds to warm the herb and release its flavors. Add the zucchini and stir to coat with oil, then shake pan to spread out zucchini. Sprinkle zucchini well with salt and let cook until starting to soften, about 2 minutes. Stir in the tomatoes and let mixture come to a boil. Reduce heat, cover, and simmer until vegetables are cooked, about 10 minutes.

Remove lid and stir in the shrimp. Cover pan again and cook until shrimp are pink, about 3 minutes. Remove from heat and divide among plates; sprinkle with the feta.

Ladle this healthy, quick, Chinese-style entrée over big bowls of steaming jasmine rice or brown rice. For best flavor, look for shrimp that haven't previously been frozen, such as rock shrimp. [SERVES 4 TO 6]

red-braised shrimp and tofu with bok choy

½ cup chicken broth

3 tablespoons soy sauce

2 tablespoons rice vinegar

1½ tablespoons ketchup

¼ to ½ teaspoon red pepper flakes

3 tablespoons vegetable oil

1 whole shallot, minced

1-inch piece fresh ginger, peeled and
   minced

1 garlic clove, minced

8 ounces firm tofu, cut into 1/2-inch cubes

6 green onions, including tops, cut into
   2-inch lengths

1½ pounds bok choy, chopped

12 ounces peeled, deveined rock shrimp or
   medium prawns

1 tablespoon cornstarch

In a measuring cup or bowl, stir together the broth, soy sauce, vinegar, and ketchup. Add the red pepper flakes to taste (¼ teaspoon for medium heat; ½ teaspoon for hot). Set sauce aside.

In a large, heavy wok or 12-inch-wide sauté pan, heat the oil over medium-high heat. When oil shimmers, add the shallot, ginger, and garlic and cook, stirring until fragrant, for 30 seconds. Add the tofu and green onions and stir until coated with aromatics. Stir in the bok choy and sauce mixture and let come to a boil, then reduce heat, cover, and simmer for 10 minutes. Stir in the shrimp, cover again, and let cook 5 minutes more.

In a small bowl, stir the cornstarch into ¼ cup water. Add to pan and cook, stirring, until sauce starts to thicken, about 1 minute. Serve immediately.

I love lunching at Hog Island Oyster Company in San Francisco's Ferry Building, looking at the bay and eating a bowl of sausage and clams. The view at home may not be as spectacular, but the food can be. Use fresh Mexican (not dried Spanish) chorizo, or substitute hot Italian sausage. While Asian fish sauce may seem out of place here, it's a trick to add depth of flavor. [SERVES 4 TO 6]

portuguese clam and sausage stew

1 tablespoon olive oil

8 ounces fresh pork chorizo

1 small yellow onion, chopped

1 garlic clove, minced

1 can (14½ ounces) chopped tomatoes

1 tablespoon Asian fish sauce (optional)

1 can (15 ounces) garbanzo beans, drained
   and rinsed

24 small hard-shell clams, scrubbed

⅓ cup chopped fresh Italian parsley leaves

In a 10- to 12-inch-wide sauté or frying pan, warm the oil over medium-high heat and crumble in the sausage meat (discard casings). Stir sausage until it breaks up and starts to brown, then add the onion. Cook, stirring, until sausage is browned and onion is softened, about 5 minutes. Add the garlic and cook for 1 minute. Stir in the tomatoes, 1 cup water, and fish sauce (if using), then add the beans. Let come to a boil, then reduce heat, cover, and simmer until thickened slightly, about 15 minutes.

Add the clams and shake pan to coat clams with sauce; increase heat to medium. Cover pan and cook until clams open, about 10 minutes (discard any that do not open). Stir in the parsley and serve.

Scallops can be braised in much the same way as meat—quickly browned and deglazed to form a wonderful sauce—but it only takes minutes, so watch the clock closely. While this sauce is good enough to eat with shoe leather, offer Golden Pilaf (page 118), orzo pasta, or toasted bread to soak up every bit. [SERVES 4]

spanish scallops

⅓ cup Romesco Sauce (page 129)

1½ pounds sea scallops

2 tablespoons olive oil

1 tablespoon butter

1 whole shallot, minced

½ cup dry white wine, such as Sauvignon Blanc

⅓ cup heavy cream

Kosher salt

Make the romesco sauce up to 3 days ahead.

One by one, pull opaque tissue or "foot" off the side of each scallop and discard. Rinse scallops and pat dry with paper towels. Warm the oil and butter in a 10- to 12-inch-wide sauté pan or frying pan over medium-high heat. When foam subsides, put scallops in pan in a single layer. Cook, without stirring, until golden brown on the bottom, about 1 minute, then turn with tongs. Cook until golden brown on the other side, about 1 minute more. Transfer scallops to a plate with tongs.

Add the shallot and cook, stirring, for 1 minute. Pour in the wine and let come to a boil, stirring to release browned bits. Pour in the cream and let come to a boil; season with a good pinch of salt. Put scallops back in pan and reduce heat, cover, and simmer until opaque through, about 3 minutes. Transfer scallops with tongs to shallow bowls. Stir romesco sauce into pan sauce, then pour over scallops, and serve immediately.

Chapter 5

VEGETABLES

It's a misconception that vegetables should be cooked quickly. A squeaky-crisp steamed green bean tastes like grass; slow-cooked, it becomes rich, earthy, and complex. When choosing a vegetable to braise, there are the obvious ones, like sturdy cauliflower, potatoes, carrots, and turnips. Shelling beans are also a natural, whether they are the main ingredient or paired with greens or tomatoes. But delicate vegetables, including peas, favas, artichokes, and even lettuce, are a revelation when given some time in the pot. Slow heat completely transforms bitter chicories, such as endive and escarole, into something sweet and mild. So it's also a misconception that when you pull out the Dutch oven, your only option is meat, poultry, or seafood when the world of vegetables is there for the braising.

I first ate this superb dish in a loft in New York on a scorching July evening. Surprisingly, it was the perfect choice; the spicy broth with *harissa* (a Tunisian spice paste found at specialty food stores) actually cooled us down. If you want a vegetarian dinner, leave out the merguez. For a traditional garnish, sprinkle diced Preserved Lemons (page 135) into each bowlful.
[SERVES 6 TO 8]

vegetable couscous

3 tablespoons olive oil

2 whole shallots, minced

¼ cup minced fresh cilantro leaves

2 garlic cloves, minced

4 cups vegetable broth

1 tablespoon whole coriander seeds

3 turnips (about 10 ounces total), peeled and cut into 2-inch pieces

2 large carrots, sliced about 1 inch thick

8 ounces green beans, trimmed and cut into 1-inch lengths

2 plum (Roma) tomatoes, seeded and chopped

1 can (15 ounces) garbanzo beans, drained and rinsed

1 pound merguez (spicy lamb sausage)

2 cups couscous

Harissa (see recipe introduction)

1 Preserved Lemon (optional)

In a 5- to 7-quart Dutch oven, warm the oil over medium-high heat. Add the shallots, cilantro, and garlic and cook, stirring, for a few minutes until fragrant, then pour in the broth and let come to a boil; stir in the coriander seeds. Add the turnips, carrots, and green beans. Reduce heat to medium, cover, and let vegetables cook for 10 minutes.

Stir in the tomatoes and garbanzo beans; return to a boil, then reduce heat, cover, and simmer until green beans and turnips are tender to the bite, about 7 minutes.

Meanwhile, broil or grill the sausage until cooked through. Slice and tent with foil to keep warm. Put the couscous in a baking dish or heat-proof bowl and pour in 2 cups of boiling water; cover with foil and let sit for 5 minutes to absorb liquid. Fluff with a fork.

To serve, place a heaping spoonful of couscous in each bowl. Lift vegetables out of pot with a slotted spoon and divide among couscous bowls. For each serving, tilt pot and fill a large ladle with broth; squeeze some harissa into the broth and stir with a fork to blend (the more harissa, the hotter). Ladle harissa broth over vegetables and couscous and top with merguez. Garnish with preserved lemon peel, if using.

This is the Food Pyramid in a dish, with its allotment of vegetables, grains, just a little fat, and some protein from garbanzo beans. It's definitely *my* interpretation of the Indian original, but it owes a deep debt to Julie Sahni, whose cookbooks I have been poring over for years. Serve with Golden Pilaf (page 118) or purchased naan bread. [SERVES 6]

indian cauliflower and potato curry

1 bunch fresh cilantro

2-inch piece fresh ginger, peeled

1 serrano or jalapeño chile pepper, stemmed and seeded

1 small head cauliflower

¼ cup vegetable oil

1 small yellow onion, thinly sliced

Kosher salt

2 tablespoons curry powder, preferably Madras

1 teaspoon cumin seeds

1 teaspoon ground cumin

2 medium red potatoes (about 12 ounces total), cut into 1-inch pieces

1 can (15 ounces) garbanzo beans, drained and rinsed

1 can (14½ ounces) chopped tomatoes

12 ounces green beans, trimmed and snapped in half

Yogurt-Mint Sauce (page 131)

Trim root ends off the cilantro stems, then cut off about 2 inches of stems; reserve leaves. Cut the ginger and chile into a few pieces and put in a food processor with the cilantro stems. Whirl until finely chopped.

Core the cauliflower and break or cut into florets about 2 inches in size.

In a 5- to 7-quart Dutch oven, warm the oil over medium-high heat. Add ingredients from food processor and stir until fragrant, about 30 seconds. Add the onion and a generous pinch of salt and cook, stirring, until onion is softened, about 3 minutes. Sprinkle the curry powder, cumin seeds, and ground cumin over onions and stir until fragrant, about 10 seconds. Pour in 1 cup water, stirring to release browned bits. Add cauliflower and stir well, then stir in the potatoes, garbanzo beans, tomatoes, and green beans. Let come to a boil, stirring once or twice to coat everything. Reduce heat, cover, and simmer until vegetables are tender, about 25 minutes.

Meanwhile, trim enough leaves off remaining cilantro to measure ½ cup; set aside. Prepare yogurt-mint sauce.

When vegetables are done, remove from heat and let sit for about 10 minutes, to settle the flavors. To serve, sprinkle each portion with cilantro leaves and spoon on some yogurt sauce.

Squat *cipollini* are similar to pearl onions, but sweeter. In Italy, they are prepared *agrodolce*, or sweet-sour, in balsamic vinegar and served as an antipasto. Look for *cipollini* in gourmet grocery stores and farmers' markets. [SERVES 4]

cipollini in honey and balsamic

1 pound cipollini onions

1 bay leaf

2 tablespoons extra-virgin olive oil

Kosher salt

1 tablespoon balsamic vinegar

⅓ cup vegetable broth or chicken broth, plus more as needed

1 tablespoon honey

Bring a saucepan of water to a boil and drop in the onions; cook for 2 minutes, then drain. When cool enough to handle, slice off the root ends and tips and slip off skins (if first layer of onion skin comes off, that's fine). Set peeled onions aside.

In a small sauté pan or frying pan just large enough to hold onions in 1 layer, warm the bay leaf in the oil over medium-high heat. When oil shimmers, add onions and a pinch of salt and shake pan to coat onions with oil. Add the vinegar and let cook, shaking pan, until it almost completely evaporates (about 30 seconds), then pour in the broth and honey and shake pan again to blend. Let liquid come to a boil, then reduce heat, cover, and simmer until onions are softened, about 15 minutes (if pan is too wide, you may have to add more broth after 10 minutes). Remove lid and cook onions over high heat until sauce is reduced to a syrupy glaze. Serve hot, warm, or at room temperature.

Credit my editor's mother, Suzanne Jonath, with sharing this beloved family recipe. She prepares it traditionally with raisins; I like it Mediterranean-style with a yogurt-dill sauce.
[SERVES 6]

braised stuffed cabbage

Kosher salt

1 head green cabbage

3 tablespoons olive oil

1 yellow onion, chopped

1 pound beef bones

2 large cans (28 ounces each) chopped tomatoes

1 pound ground round or other ground beef

4 green onions, including tops, minced

2 eggs

¼ cup uncooked white rice

1 tablespoon Worcestershire sauce

Freshly ground pepper

About 2 tablespoons honey

2 to 4 tablespoons freshly squeezed lemon juice

¼ cup raisins (optional)

1 cup whole-milk yogurt (optional)

2 tablespoons chopped fresh dill (optional)

Bring a large pot of salted water to a rolling boil. Core the cabbage and drop cabbage into boiling water. Boil until leaves soften and can be separated, about 5 minutes. Lift out cabbage with tongs and drain on paper towels. Peel off 12 outer leaves and set aside (keep remaining cabbage at hand).

In a 5- to 7-quart Dutch oven, warm the oil over medium-high heat. Add the onion and cook, stirring, until softened, about 3 minutes. Add the bones and cook, turning once or twice, until lightly browned, about 5 minutes. Add the tomatoes and let come to a boil, then reduce heat, cover, and simmer for 30 minutes.

Meanwhile, in a large bowl, combine the ground beef, green onions, eggs, rice, Worcestershire sauce, 1½ teaspoons salt, and several grindings of pepper. With your hands, gently but thoroughly blend mixture until no longer wet. Scoop a scant ¼ cup of mixture, shape into an elongated ball, and place on a cooked cabbage leaf, setting about 2 inches from the top of the leaf. Fold top of leaf over filling, fold in sides, then carefully roll up. Place stuffed cabbage seam side down and continue with remaining meat and leaves. With tongs, transfer stuffed leaves to pot with tomato sauce, snuggling in so just submerged (you can pull out a bone to make room). Cover pot and simmer for 1 hour.

Stir the honey, 2 tablespoons of the lemon juice, and raisins, if using, into the sauce, then cover and simmer 30 minutes more. Turn off heat and let sit for 10 to 15 minutes before serving, to settle flavors. Taste sauce and adjust as needed with more honey and lemon juice to balance flavors before serving.

Alternatively, leave out raisins and once cabbage leaves have cooked, stir together remaining 2 tablespoons of the lemon juice, yogurt, and dill. Place 2 stuffed leaves on each plate, ladle tomato sauce around them, then drizzle with yogurt mixture.

The Italians often braise Swiss chard with beans for a humble and healthy sauce over pasta. I like to serve this meatless stew over rice or polenta. For best texture, I don't use the chard stems, setting them aside for minestrone or to braise on their own. [SERVES 6]

swiss chard with cannellini

1 bunch (about 1 pound) red, white, or rainbow Swiss chard

¼ cup olive oil

1 yellow onion, chopped

1 celery stalk, chopped

1 carrot, chopped

2 garlic cloves, roughly chopped

1 can (14½ ounces) chopped tomatoes

¼ teaspoon red pepper flakes

1 can (15 ounces) cannellini beans, drained and rinsed

Kosher salt

Freshly ground pepper

Trim the stems and center ribs off the chard and reserve for another use. Rinse leaves, shake off excess water, and stack leaves on a cutting board. Thinly slice crosswise. Set aside.

In a 10- to 12-inch-wide sauté pan or 5- to 7-quart Dutch oven, warm the oil over medium-high heat and add the onion, celery, and carrot. Cook, stirring, until vegetables are softened, about 5 minutes. Stir in the garlic and cook for about 30 seconds until fragrant, then stir in the tomatoes and red pepper flakes. Reduce heat and simmer, uncovered, until tomatoes break down and sauce thickens a bit, about 10 minutes. Stir in chard by the handful, letting each addition cook down a bit before adding the next. Stir in the beans. Cover pan and simmer until greens are very soft, 10 to 15 minutes more. Season to taste with salt and pepper.

This is the simplest recipe in this book, but it epitomizes the elegance of braising: By slow-cooking bitter escarole in its own juice, it takes on an improbably sweet, succulent character. Escarole is a member of the chicory family and resembles butter lettuce but with bigger, darker leaves. If you can't find escarole, Swiss chard leaves and stems can be braised in the same way.
[SERVES 4]

braised escarole

1 head (about 1 pound) escarole
2 tablespoons butter
1 tablespoon olive oil
2 green onions, including tops, thinly sliced
Kosher salt
½ lemon, juiced
Freshly ground pepper

Trim core from the escarole, then chop leaves. Rinse leaves well in a colander, shaking lightly to rid of excess water.

In a 10- to 12-inch-wide sauté pan or 5- to 7-quart Dutch oven over medium-high heat, melt the butter in the oil. Add the onions and cook, stirring, for 1 minute. Add escarole, then cover pot and let cook until escarole starts to wilt down, about 5 minutes. Uncover and sprinkle escarole with a generous pinch of salt. Stir until all the leaves wilt, then reduce heat, cover, and simmer until escarole is tender, about 20 minutes. Turn off heat and add lemon juice to escarole; season well with pepper.

Soybeans—sold in markets as "edamame"—are a great choice for braising because they hold their texture as they absorb flavors. For the best taste, use fresh edamame and corn; if frozen vegetables are all that is available, thaw only partially before using. [SERVES 4]

bean and corn stew with bacon

2 strips thick (butcher) bacon

1 whole shallot, sliced

½ teaspoon dried thyme leaves

2 cups shelled edamame

2 cups (2 cobs) fresh corn kernels

Kosher salt

⅓ cup apple cider vinegar

Kat Daddy's Pepper Vinegar (page 132) or hot pepper sauce, such as Tabasco

Cut the bacon lengthwise in half, then crosswise into small pieces. Put bacon in a 10- to 12-inch-wide sauté pan or frying pan set over medium-high heat. Cook, stirring, until bacon is golden brown (but not crisp) and fat is rendered, about 5 minutes. Add the shallot and thyme and cook, stirring, until shallot starts to soften, about 1 minute. Pour in ½ cup water, stirring to release browned bits. Add the edamame, corn, and a generous pinch of salt. Bring to a boil, then reduce heat, cover, and simmer until vegetables are cooked through, about 10 minutes.

Remove lid from pan and increase heat to high. Cook, stirring, until any liquid in pan has evaporated, then pour in the apple cider vinegar. Let boil for 1 minute, shaking pan often, then remove from heat and season to taste with pepper vinegar.

I'm a shell-bean freak. In spring, I can't wait for the coming of favas in their parka-like pods, or in fall for the arrival of borlotti in their mottled-maroon jackets. Poking my thumbnail into a seam and unzipping the shell from top to bottom, then trailing the beans into a bowl, is a ritual that connects me with generations of cooks for whom beans were a life-sustaining, cheap protein.

Consider this recipe a starting point; you could add chopped bacon or pancetta with the onion, fresh tomatoes and any number of herbs with the broth, or fresh spinach at the end. Top the beans with a streak of olive oil and salt, as done here, or with shavings of Parmesan, pecorino, or ricotta salata cheese. Beans are a canvas; make of them whatever art you feel.

[SERVES 4]

braised borlotti beans

Extra-virgin olive oil

1 cup chopped red onion

1 carrot, chopped

1 celery stalk, chopped

1½ pounds fresh borlotti or cranberry beans, shelled (about 2 cups)

1½ to 2 cups vegetable broth or chicken broth

6 sprigs fresh Italian parsley, plus ¼ cup chopped parsley leaves

1 bay leaf

Kosher salt

Lemon-Rosemary Salt (page 133; optional)

In an 8- to 10-inch-wide sauté pan or frying pan, warm 3 tablespoons of the oil over medium-high heat. Add the onion, carrot, and celery, and cook, stirring often, until softened, about 5 minutes. Stir in the beans, then pour in 1½ cups of the broth and let come to a boil. Lay the parsley sprigs and bay leaf in center of pan over beans, reduce heat, cover, and simmer until beans are tender, 45 to 50 minutes, checking after 30 minutes and pouring in more broth if all the liquid has already been absorbed (shake pan to distribute rather than stirring so you don't mix in the herbs). Discard parsley and bay leaf.

Remove beans from heat and season lightly with kosher salt. Stir the chopped parsley into beans. Serve beans hot, warm, or at room temperature, drizzling each portion with a little olive oil and sprinkling with a pinch of the lemon-rosemary salt, if using.

The whole point of this dish is generosity: Be generous with the oil, be generous with the salt, be generous with the cooking time. You can make it with regular green beans, but part of the allure is waiting for fat, flat Romanos (sometimes called Italian beans) to come into season late spring through early fall. Then you would be wise to serve this as often as possible.

[SERVES 4]

tomato-braised romano beans

1 pound Romano beans

1 garlic clove

¼ cup extra-virgin olive oil

Kosher salt

1 cup seeded and diced peeled tomatoes
  (fresh or canned)

Snap stem off each bean then break bean into 2-inch lengths. Whack the garlic with the side of a chef's knife and remove peel. In a 10- to 12-inch-wide sauté pan or frying pan over medium-high heat, warm garlic in the oil, shaking pan a few times to flavor oil. When garlic starts to color, add beans and a generous pinch of salt and cook, stirring occasionally, until beans turn a deeper green and start to blister, 3 to 4 minutes. Stir in the tomatoes. Let come to a boil, then reduce heat, cover, and simmer until beans are very tender and sauce is glossy, about 30 minutes, stirring once or twice. Discard garlic before serving.

This delicate dish pays homage to my French training at Tante Marie's Cooking School. It also proves there's more to lettuce than carrying olive oil and vinegar to the mouth. Rinse the leaves just before cooking; the water that clings to them becomes the braising liquid. [SERVES 4]

butter-braised lettuce with fresh peas and thyme

1 head romaine lettuce (about 1 pound)

4 green onions

4 tablespoons butter

½ teaspoon kosher salt

1 pound fresh peas in the pod, shelled (about 1 cup)

½ teaspoon sugar

6 sprigs fresh thyme

Separate the lettuce into leaves, trimming off any darkened ends or brown-tinged tips. Rinse leaves and shake off excess water. Stack leaves and cut crosswise into thirds. Cut the onions, including tops, into ¼-inch-thick slices.

In a 10- to 12-inch-wide sauté pan or frying pan over medium heat, melt the butter. Add onions and cook, stirring once or twice, for 1 minute. Add lettuce and sprinkle with the salt. Cover pan and let cook until lettuce starts to wilt, 2 or 3 minutes. Stir in the peas and sugar, then shake pan to spread out vegetables. Lay the thyme sprigs on top. Cover pan again and cook until peas and lettuce are sweet and tender, about 10 minutes. Remove thyme sprigs before serving.

The compact shape of endives means they are great for braising, which in turn makes them much sweeter. If you've never cooked endive, the flavor and texture will be a revelation.
[SERVES 4]

pan-braised endive with crusty cheese

4 large Belgian endives

2 tablespoons butter

1 tablespoon olive oil

1 whole shallot, minced

½ to 1 cup vegetable broth or chicken broth

Kosher salt

½ cup freshly grated Parmesan cheese

Freshly ground pepper

Cut each endive in half lengthwise. In an 8- to 10-inch-wide sauté pan or ovenproof frying pan just large enough to hold endive halves in 1 layer, melt the butter in the oil over medium-high heat. Add the shallot and cook, stirring, until softened, about 2 minutes. Arrange endives, cut sides down, in 1 layer in pan. Pour in enough of the broth to measure ¼ inch deep; let come to a boil. Sprinkle endives with salt, then reduce heat, cover, and simmer until endives are soft when pierced, about 20 minutes. Preheat a broiler.

Uncover pan and turn endives over. Sprinkle tops of endives with the cheese, then grind pepper over cheese. Put pan in broiler and cook until cheese is bubbly and golden brown; it's okay if the edges of endives brown slightly. Remove from broiler and let endives sit a minute or two to cool off before serving.

If you like bright green, squeaky-crisp beans, this recipe may not be for you. But if you want to taste how rich green beans can be—even if they turn olive-drab in color—braise them. You can substitute kosher salt if you don't have the flavored salt on hand, but it's worth making it for this and many other recipes in this book. [SERVES 4]

slow-cooked green beans with dill

2 tablespoons extra-virgin olive oil

1 whole shallot, minced

1 garlic clove, minced

1 pound green beans, trimmed and snapped in half

2 teaspoons Lemon-Rosemary Salt (page 133)

2 tablespoons chopped fresh dill

In an 8- to 10-inch-wide sauté pan or frying pan, warm the oil with the shallot and garlic over medium-high heat, stirring. When shallot and garlic start to sizzle, add the beans along with the salt and shake pan vigorously to coat beans with oil (or stir well with a large spoon). Cook beans, stirring, until skins start to deepen in color, about 2 minutes. Pour in 1 cup water and let come to a boil. Reduce heat, cover, and simmer until beans are very tender, 15 to 20 minutes. Remove from heat and stir in the dill.

I'll never forget walking down a street in Rome and seeing a tableful of men under the morning sun, shelling fava beans and gossiping. They were getting ready to make *vignarola*, the town's famous homage to spring. Because it is labor-intensive, I make this for just two people, but it can be doubled, tripled, or increased in any measure if you have some friends on hand to shell beans with you—and gossip. [SERVES 2]

spring stew of favas, artichokes, and fresh peas (la vignarola)

1 pound fresh fava beans

Kosher salt

1 pound fresh peas in the pod, shelled (about 1 cup)

1 lemon

12 small or "baby" artichokes or 3 large artichokes

3 tablespoons extra-virgin olive oil

3 spring onion bulbs or whole shallots, chopped

2 tablespoons minced fresh mint leaves

Shell the fava beans. Bring a small pan of salted water to a boil and drop in shelled beans; cook for 20 seconds, then drain. Let cool for a minute, then slit each bean with a small sharp knife and squeeze gently to pop out inner beans into a small bowl. Put the peas in another bowl.

Fill a third bowl with water and squeeze the lemon into it; then drop it in. Working with 1 small artichoke at a time, tear off the dark green leaves to reach the tender yellow leaves. With a small sharp knife, pare away any tough green patches of leaf from the bottom, then trim off the sharp tips. Cut each artichoke in half. (If using large artichokes, peel down to the heart, scoop out the fuzzy choke, and cut each heart into quarters.) Drop each artichoke into bowl of lemon water as it is prepared, to prevent discoloring.

In a 10- to 12-inch-wide sauté pan or frying pan, warm the oil over medium-high heat. Add the onions and cook, stirring, until softened, about 2 minutes. Lift artichokes out of lemon water with a slotted spoon and add to pan; season with a generous pinch of salt and add ¼ cup water; when it comes to a boil, turn heat to medium-low and cover pan. Let artichokes cook for 5 minutes, then stir in peas and 2 tablespoons water. Cover and cook for 5 more minutes, then stir in fava beans and 2 more tablespoons water. Cover and cook until all the vegetables are tender, about 10 minutes. Stir in the mint, season to taste with salt, and remove from heat. Serve hot, warm, or at room temperature.

Chapter 6

ACCOMPANIMENTS

You dip a ladle into the pot, scooping up tender chunks of meat and onions; a curl of fragrant steam rises from the sauce. But what to serve with your braise? The answer is in this chapter. There are quick recipes for starches to go underneath, including buttery noodles with herbs, killer mashed potatoes with cheese, shortcut versions of polenta and risotto, and a rice pilaf that complements everything. There are also recipes for condiments and toppings— little bursts of flavor to sprinkle over and around braises and stews. Hot pepper vinegar is the ticket to crank up the heat, horseradish cream is for meat lovers, and herby gremolata is as habit-forming as salt. Speaking of salt, every good cook should have a batch of Lemon-Rosemary Salt to finesse her cooking; keep a jarful on hand in your pantry. Now that you know what to put under, and over, your braises and stews, just add a glass of wine and enjoy.

This is the essential accompaniment for Moroccan Lamb Tagine (page 55), but it's also great with Winter Market Chicken (page 64), and Persian Chicken (page 71). Look for plump Turkish apricots in health food stores or well-stocked supermarkets; they aren't as leathery as the California dried fruit. For an elegant touch, stir in ½ cup toasted slivered almonds at the end. [SERVES 6]

apricot couscous

2 cups couscous
½ cup diced dried apricots
   (preferably Turkish)
½ teaspoon salt

In a medium baking dish or heat-proof bowl, stir together the couscous and apricots. Mix 3 cups boiling water and the salt in a measuring cup. Pour over couscous and immediately cover dish with foil. Let stand until liquid is absorbed, about 5 minutes. Remove foil and fluff couscous with a fork. If you need to keep it warm, put couscous, covered with foil, in a low oven until ready to serve.

Polenta is the perfect base for many braises, especially short ribs (pages 25 and 28), Stracotto (page 33), and meat or chicken stews. But stirring polenta for forty minutes isn't much fun, so this shortcut uses the oven, which you might already have on to cook your braised dish. Use coarse-ground yellow polenta, not quick-cooking, for this recipe. [SERVES 4 TO 6]

creamy baked polenta

2 tablespoons butter, plus additional
    for buttering dish
2½ cups milk
½ teaspoon salt
1 cup coarse-ground yellow polenta

Preheat an oven to 350 degrees F. Generously butter the bottom and sides of an 8-inch square baking dish.

Combine the milk, 2½ cups water, butter, and salt in a saucepan and place over medium-high heat until butter melts and liquid is steaming. Whisk in the polenta, then reduce heat to medium. Continue to whisk until mixture thickens to a porridge-like consistency and large bubbles break the surface, 6 to 8 minutes.

Remove from heat and pour polenta into buttered baking dish. Cut a piece of parchment paper slightly larger than the baking dish and butter 1 side of it generously. Place parchment on top of polenta, buttered side down, pressing onto surface of polenta; fold in edges of paper so there is no overhang. Bake until liquid is absorbed, about 20 minutes, then remove from oven and let polenta stand, with parchment on, for 10 minutes before serving.

This universal dish pairs with almost every meat, poultry, and fish recipe in this book. Use basmati rice for a fragrant, nutty variation that's especially good with Indian or Asian dishes. If you need rice for more people, increase ingredients proportionately. [SERVES 6]

golden pilaf

1 tablespoon butter

1 tablespoon vegetable oil

1 small onion, finely chopped

¼ teaspoon saffron threads

1½ cups long-grain white rice

3 cups chicken broth

¼ teaspoon kosher salt

In a medium saucepan, melt the butter in the oil over medium-high heat. Add the onion and saffron and cook, stirring, until onion is softened, about 3 minutes. Add the rice and stir until coated with fat, about 30 seconds. Pour in the broth and add the salt; let come to a boil. Reduce heat, cover, and simmer until liquid is just absorbed, about 20 minutes. Turn off heat and let rice sit, undisturbed, for 10 minutes. Fluff with a fork and serve.

I may have embraced *farro* on my table only in recent years, but the Italians have been enjoying it since Roman times. A lightly milled form of hard wheat, it looks, tastes, and chews a lot like barley, but is more satisfying. It can be served with most braises you'd serve with rice, including Veal with Mushrooms (page 34), Osso Buco (page 36), or Coq au Vin (page 62). Look for farro in Italian food stores or gourmet groceries. Semiperlato is the most common form and the best for this recipe. [SERVES 6]

farrotto

3 tablespoons olive oil

1 small yellow onion, finely chopped

2 celery stalks, finely chopped

1 carrot, finely chopped

Kosher salt

1½ cups farro

3 cups chicken broth

In an 8- to 10-inch-wide sauté pan or frying pan, warm the oil over medium-high heat. Add the onion, celery, carrot, and a generous pinch of salt. Cook, stirring, until vegetables are tender, about 10 minutes. Meanwhile, rinse the farro in a fine sieve and shake well to get rid of excess water.

Add farro to pan and stir to coat with oil. Pour in 2 cups of the broth and let come to a boil. Reduce heat, cover, and simmer until broth is almost absorbed, about 20 minutes. Stir in remaining broth, let come to a boil again, then reduce heat, cover, and simmer until farro is still chewy, but no longer starchy, about 20 minutes more.

I suspect a lot of us grew up with plain egg noodles, not fancy pasta, under our stews. While it may have seemed boring then, revisit the idea now, seasoning the noodles with delicious olive oil and a fistful of herbs. Serve with Classic Pot Roast (page 20), Tuscan Chicken Stew (page 70), Sicilian Swordfish (page 85), or Greek Lamb Meatballs (page 58), to name just a few. You can also add just about any other fresh herbs you have on hand. [SERVES 6]

herbed wide noodles

Kosher salt

12 ounces wide egg noodles

1 cup loosely packed fresh Italian parsley leaves, minced

½ cup loosely packed fresh basil leaves, minced

2 tablespoons minced fresh chives

2 tablespoons butter

2 tablespoons extra-virgin olive oil

Bring a stockpot or pasta pot of salted water to a rolling boil. Drop in the noodles and cook according to package directions. Meanwhile, stir together the parsley, basil, and chives.

When noodles are done, drain in a colander. Put the butter and oil in the bottom of pot that you cooked pasta in, then return noodles to pot (do not turn on heat). Toss noodles until coated with melted butter and oil. Season with salt, then stir in the herbs and serve.

Serve this as the underpinning to Osso Buco (page 36), Veal Braised in Milk (page 35), or with vegetables, such as Romano Beans (page 107) or Braised Escarole (page 104). For a great match with Beef Stew with Onions (page 30), substitute crumbled blue cheese for the Parmesan. [SERVES 4 TO 6]

shortcut risotto

3½ cups vegetable broth or chicken broth

3 tablespoons olive oil

1 yellow onion, chopped

1½ cups Arborio rice

½ cup dry white wine or vermouth

½ cup freshly grated Parmesan cheese

In a small saucepan, bring the broth to a boil, then reduce heat to low and keep warm on a back burner while you make the risotto. Place a ladle with at least a ½-cup capacity nearby.

In a 10- to 12-inch-wide sauté pan or ovenproof frying pan, warm the oil over medium-high heat. Add the onion and cook, stirring, until softened, about 3 minutes. Add the rice and stir until coated with oil, about 30 seconds. Pour in the wine, stirring until it almost evaporates. Ladle in ½ cup of simmering broth, stirring until it just evaporates, then add another ½ cup. Repeat until you have used 2 cups broth; total cooking time will be about 8 minutes.

Stir in 1 cup of remaining broth, let come to a boil, then reduce heat, cover, and cook until rice is just tender and liquid is absorbed, about 12 minutes. Stir in remaining broth and the cheese, then remove from heat. Cover and let risotto stand for 5 minutes before serving.

When making mashed potatoes, be sure to use baking, or Idaho, potatoes, which are the starchiest. If you don't have a potato masher, a sturdy metal whisk (but not a balloon whisk) will work. Serve this with Pub Short Ribs (page 28), Classic Pot Roast (page 20), Braised "Barbecue" Brisket (page 22), or with Romano Beans (page 107) for a vegetarian meal.

[SERVES 6]

cheddar mashers

3 baking potatoes (about 1½ pounds total)
Kosher salt
2 tablespoons butter
2 green onions, including tops, finely chopped
⅓ to ½ cup regular or low-fat milk
1 cup (4 ounces) grated sharp cheddar cheese
Freshly ground pepper

Peel the potatoes, rinse, and cut into 1-inch cubes. Put potatoes in a pot with water just to cover, then add 2 teaspoons salt. Place over high heat and boil potatoes until a piece collapses when pushed against the side of the pot with a spoon, about 20 minutes.

Pour potatoes into a colander and leave in sink for a few minutes to eliminate excess water and steam.

Put the butter and onions in pot used for potatoes and set over medium heat; stir until butter melts, then return potatoes to pot, add ⅓ cup of the milk and the cheese, and mash with a potato masher or heavy whisk, blending until fairly smooth (if mixture looks dry, add more milk, a few tablespoons at a time). Turn off heat and season with salt and pepper.

The secret to this coleslaw—the specialty of the lovely mother-in-law of a close friend—is briny capers and their juice; the end result is far more sophisticated than the standard picnic dish. Offer as a crisp contrast to stews or chili, stuff into tortillas with Carnitas (page 43), or serve on buns with sliced Braised "Barbecue" Brisket (page 22). If you don't want to hand-shred cabbage, use bagged shredded cabbage, as long as it is impeccably fresh. [SERVES 6]

naneita's coleslaw

1 head green cabbage, halved, cored, and finely shredded (about 1 pound)
1 cup fresh Italian parsley leaves, coarsely chopped
3 green onions, including tops, thinly sliced
⅓ cup mayonnaise
¼ cup freshly squeezed lemon juice
¼ cup capers
2 tablespoons caper juice
Kosher salt

Put the cabbage, parsley, and onions in a large bowl. In a small bowl, whisk the mayonnaise and lemon juice until smooth. Pour over cabbage mixture. Add the capers and caper juice and toss well. Cover bowl with plastic wrap and refrigerate for at least ½ hour or up to 3 hours (coleslaw will get moister as it sits). Season with salt and mix well just before serving.

This Spanish condiment has become as popular as aioli was a few years ago. It can be used as an ingredient in Spanish Scallops (page 92) or as a condiment for other braises. Stir a spoonful into stews or spread on toasted baguette and offer alongside Cipollini in Honey and Balsamic (page 99). Pimentón is smoked Spanish paprika, and you can find it in specialty food stores and some supermarkets. [MAKES 1 GENEROUS CUP]

romesco sauce

4 garlic cloves, unpeeled

2 plum (Roma) tomatoes

1 small red bell pepper

½ cup slivered almonds

1 slice whole wheat toast

1 tablespoon sherry vinegar or
   red wine vinegar

1 teaspoon pimentón or paprika

1 teaspoon kosher salt

2 tablespoons extra-virgin olive oil

Preheat an oven to 350 degrees F. Wrap the garlic in foil. Place the tomatoes, bell pepper, and garlic packet on an ungreased baking sheet and roast in the oven for 30 minutes. Remove garlic packet and tomatoes and set aside; turn pepper over with tongs and return to oven. Spread the almonds on a pie plate and place in oven. Roast pepper and almonds for 10 more minutes, then remove.

Pull skins off tomatoes and discard; cut tomatoes in half and squeeze or scrape out seeds. Cut bell pepper in half and remove stem, seeds, and ribs. Peel garlic. In a food processor fitted with the metal blade, combine tomatoes, bell pepper, garlic, and almonds. Pulse until finely chopped, then add the toast (torn into pieces), vinegar, pimentón, and salt, and pulse until blended. Add the oil through the feed tube, processing until sauce is blended, but not perfectly smooth. Transfer to a bowl and serve at room temperature or store, covered, in the refrigerator for up to 4 days.

This is the traditional condiment to serve with Classic Pot Roast (page 20), Stracotto (page 33), Pub Short Ribs (page 28), or Lamb Shanks (page 52). [MAKES ⅔ CUP]

horseradish cream

½ cup sour cream

2 tablespoons prepared horseradish

Kosher salt

Freshly ground pepper

In a small bowl, stir together the sour cream and horseradish and season with salt and pepper. Serve, or cover and refrigerate up to 1 day.

Spoon this over Greek Lamb Meatballs (page 58) or Cauliflower and Potato Curry (page 98), or as an alternative topping to Braised Stuffed Cabbage (page 100). Be sure to use whole-milk yogurt; if made with low-fat or nonfat yogurt, it lacks oompf. [MAKES 1¼ CUPS]

yogurt-mint sauce

1 cup (8 ounces) whole-milk plain yogurt

2 tablespoons freshly squeezed lemon juice

2 tablespoons finely chopped fresh mint leaves

1 garlic clove, minced

½ teaspoon kosher salt

In a small bowl, stir together all the ingredients until smooth. Serve, or cover and refrigerate up to 1 day.

In the South, this is used to season braised greens, meats, barbecue, beans, and whatever else you might want to spice up a bit. It's very easy and fun to make at home. For a pretty bottle, buy French sparkling lemonade in a 750-ml glass bottle with a self-stopper. Once you've consumed the lemonade, wash the bottle very well with hot, soapy water, remove labels, then sterilize bottle with boiling water or run it through the dishwasher cycle.

[MAKES ABOUT 3½ CUPS]

kat daddy's pepper vinegar

8 serrano chiles

3⅓ cups (750 ml) white wine vinegar

1 tablespoon sugar

Rinse the chiles and pat dry with paper towels. Stuff chiles into a clean, sterilized 750-ml bottle (see recipe introduction), slitting the sides of 2 or 3 of them to let extra heat come through (if the chiles jam in the bottle neck, push through with a skewer). In a saucepan, heat the vinegar and sugar just to the boiling point; pour through a funnel into bottle. Close bottle with stopper. Store vinegar in a cool, dark place for 3 weeks before use. Vinegar keeps for up to 3 months.

Adapted from Susan Hermann Loomis's recipe in the *Italian Farmhouse Cookbook,* this salt has become the secret weapon in my kitchen. It makes the flavors of everything pop, which is why it is called for in recipes throughout this book. You'll find lots of other ways to use it, too, such as seasoning lamb and pork chops, and for the world's best roast chicken (the recipe for which is in Susan's book). [MAKES ABOUT ½ CUP]

lemon-rosemary salt

2 lemons

2 tablespoons roughly chopped fresh
  rosemary leaves

1 large or 2 small garlic cloves

½ cup sea salt

Pare the zest off the lemons with a zesting tool or grater. In a food processor, combine the rosemary, garlic, and zest. Whirl until finely chopped. Add the salt and pulse once or twice to mix. Store in a cool dark place in an airtight glass jar for up to 2 months.

Think of this as a seasoning like salt: It pumps up flavors (without any sodium of course) and you use it sparingly. Sprinkle over Osso Buco (page 36), Pappardelle with Ragù (page 56), or Stracotto (page 33). Mix any extra gremolata with hot pasta or into Herbed Wide Noodles (page 121), or even stir it into Shortcut Risotto (page 123). [SERVES 6]

basil gremolata

2 lemons

1 garlic clove

3 tablespoons minced fresh basil leaves

1 tablespoon minced fresh Italian parsley leaves

Remove the zest of the lemons with a zester that cuts it off in thin strips, if you have one. Slice the garlic, then combine zest and garlic on a cutting board and mince together. Transfer to a small bowl. (If you do not have a zester tool, just grate zest and mince garlic separately, then combine them.) Stir in the basil and parsley and serve.

This is *the* Moroccan condiment, so it's a must for Lamb Tagine (page 55) or Vegetable Couscous (page 96). I also sprinkle preserved lemons on vegetable braises, like Green Beans with Dill (page 110) or Swiss Chard with Cannellini (page 103), for a citrusy, salty note. They need to be made at least three weeks ahead, but are a cinch to prepare. When serving, scrape away the pulp and dice the peel; that's the part you eat. [MAKES 1 PINT]

preserved lemons

About 12 organically grown lemons,
  preferably Meyer
Kosher salt
2 fresh or dried bay leaves

Sterilize a 1-pint glass canning jar and lid.

Cut 6 of the lemons, 1 by 1, into quarters through 1 end without cutting all the way through other end—you want lemon to open out like a flower, but not to separate. Place cut lemon on a piece of parchment or waxed paper, spread quarters open and sprinkle flesh with a heaping tablespoon of salt; put lemon into jar.

Continue with remaining lemons, sprinkling salt on each one. Pack lemons in jar tightly, filling it to the top (you may need more or less than 6 lemons, depending on their size). When finished, lift the parchment and pour the excess salt from it into jar.

Slide the bay leaves down the insides of the jar, placing on opposite sides. Juice remaining lemons 1 by 1, adding juice to jar until it reaches the top. Seal jar, shake well, and let stand at room temperature, shaking well every 12 hours, for 1 week. After 1 week, transfer jar to the refrigerator. Lemons are ready to use after 2 more weeks and keep up to 3 months in the refrigerator. To use lemons, pull out a lemon quarter and scrape away pulp. Dice peel and serve as directed.

(recipe titles are abbreviated)

	PAGE	COUSCOUS	POLENTA	PILAF	NOODLES	FARROTTO	RISOTTO	MASHERS	COLESLAW
Asian-Style Short Ribs	25		x	x					
Bean and Corn Stew	105								x
Beef Stew with Onions	30			x	x	x	x		
Borlotti Beans	106		x	x		x			
Bouillabaisse	80			x		x			
Braised "Barbeque" Brisket	22		x					x	x
Braised Escarole	104			x		x	x		
Braised Stuffed Cabbage	100							x	
Butter-Braised Lettuce	108			x		x			
Carnitas	43			x					x
Cauliflower and Potato Curry	98			x					
Chicken Bouillabaisse	63					x			
Chicken Cacciatore	72		x	x	x	x	x	x	
Chicken with Escarole, Lemon, and Olives	67			x	x	x	x		
Chili Colorado	46			x					x
Cipollini in Honey and Balsamic	99					x			
Clam and Sausage Stew	91			x					
Classic Pot Roast	20			x	x		x	x	
Coconut-Chicken Curry	69			x					
Coq au Vin	62			x	x	x		x	
Game Hens in a Pot	76			x		x			
Ginger-Braised Spareribs	49			x					
Greek Lamb Meatballs	58			x	x	x			
Greek Shrimp	88			x		x			
Green Beans with Dill	110			x		x			
Greens with Ham*	59								
Harvest Pork Stew	45	x	x	x					

	PAGE	COUSCOUS	POLENTA	PILAF	NOODLES	FARROTTO	RISOTTO	MASHERS	COLESLAW
Lamb Shanks	52		x						
Lamb Stew with Artichokes	51			x	x	x	x		
Lamb Tagine	55	x							
Monday Night Chili	27		x	x					x
Osso Buco	36		x			x	x		
Pan-Braised Endive	109			x		x			
Pappardelle with Ragù	56				x				
Persian Chicken	71	x		x					
Pork Stew with Tomatillos	42			x					
Pub Short Ribs	28		x		x			x	x
Red-Braised Shrimp and Tofu	89			x					
Rich Red Cowboy Stew	32		x					x	x
Romano Beans	107					x	x	x	
Salmon Ragout	84			x	x				
Sausages with Lentils	50			x					
Sicilian Swordfish	85			x	x	x			
Spanish Scallops	92			x		x			
Spring Stew (La Vignarola)	113					x			
Stracotto	33		x		x	x	x		
Summer Stew	83			x					
Swiss Chard with Cannellini	103		x			x			
Thai Fish Curry	86			x					
True Chili Verde	47			x					
Turkey Posole	73								x
Turkey Pot Pie	74								x
Tuscan Chicken Stew	70				x	x	x		
Veal Braised in Milk	35			x		x	x		
Veal Paprikas	38			x	x	x			
Veal with Mushrooms	34			x	x	x	x		
Vegetable Couscous*	96								
Winter Market Chicken	64	x		x					

*recipe incorporates a grain

index

table of equivalents

The exact equivalents in the following tables have been rounded for convenience.

LIQUID/DRY MEASURES

U.S.	METRIC
¼ teaspoon	1.25 milliliters
½ teaspoon	2.5 milliliters
1 teaspoon	5 milliliters
1 tablespoon (3 teaspoons)	15 milliliters
1 fluid ounce (2 tablespoons)	30 milliliters
¼ cup	60 milliliters
⅓ cup	80 milliliters
½ cup	120 milliliters
1 cup	240 milliliters
1 pint (2 cups)	480 milliliters
1 quart (4 cups, 32 ounces)	960 milliliters
1 gallon (4 quarts)	3.84 liters
1 ounce (by weight)	28 grams
1 pound	454 grams
2.2 pounds	1 kilogram

OVEN TEMPERATURE

FAHRENHEIT	CELSIUS	GAS
250	120	½
275	140	1
300	150	2
325	160	3
350	180	4
375	190	5
400	200	6
425	220	7
450	230	8
475	240	9
500	260	10

LENGTH

U.S.	METRIC
⅛ inch	3 millimeters
¼ inch	6 millimeters
½ inch	12 millimeters
1 inch	2.5 centimeters